W9-CXY-758

What they said about the 1976 edition of
What Do You Do With A Kinkajou?

"An extraordinary book! . . . Cee has to be real, for no one could invent her. She is unforgettable, and many of her adventures are hilarious."
— Gladys Taber

"Everyone knows at least one animal collector - someone who accumulates numerous cats or dogs, which gradually take over the owner's home and lifestyle. . . . Caring for this menagerie becomes a full-time occupation, humorously described. . . ."
— *Library Journal*

"Animal lovers surely will find the story rewarding both in the hilarious antics of the mistress and her menagerie and in the unremitting labor and deep-felt love she gives her charges."
— *The Kansas City Star*

"*Kinkajou* could become the most popular volume in Littleton since Ralph Moody gave us *Little Britches* and *Man of the Family*."
— *The Littleton Independent*

"A book to satisfy the secret fantasies of all animal lovers."
— *Kirkus Reviews*

Alice Wolf Gilborn

What Do You Do With a Kinkajou?

The Blueline Press
Blue Mountain Lake
New York

For Craig
For all reasons

First published in the United States by J. B. Lippincott Company 1976
Large print edition by G. K. Hall & Co. 1976
Popular Library edition 1977
New and expanded edition published by The Blueline Press,
Blue Mountain Lake, New York 1988

Library of Congress Catalog Card Number: 88-80685

ISBN: 0-9620309-0-2 (previously ISBN: 0-397-01109-1)

Cover design by Jane Mackintosh
Photographs by Bruce Wolf and Craig Gilborn
New material typeset by Countryside Typography
Set in Baskerville and Bodoni Bold
Printed in the United States of America
by Thomson-Shore Inc., Dexter, MI

Willowcroft

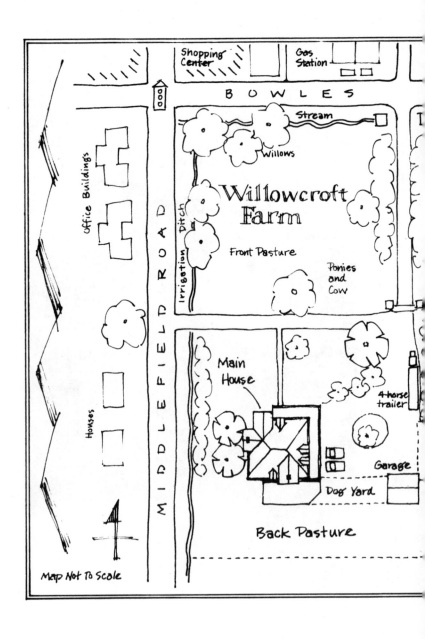

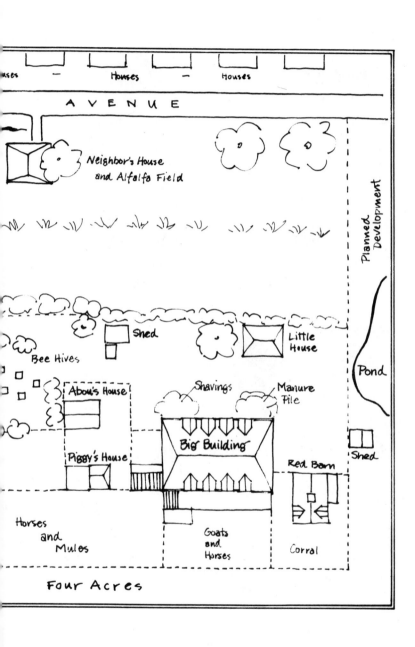

Houses — Houses — Houses

A V E N U E

Neighbor's House
and Alfalfa Field

Planned Development

Shed

Little House

Bee Hives

Abou's House

Shavings

Manure Pile

Big Building

Pond

Shed

Piggy's House

Red Barn

Horses and Mules

Goats and Horses

Corral

Four Acres

Pecking order

Contents

Cee and Harry, 1976

1

Flying West

REVISITING THE LAND of one's childhood can be a jolt to the system, even if the trip home is not simply a journey of the imagination but an actual routine occurrence. Though I had returned to Colorado every summer since 1960, when my husband, Craig, and I had moved East, I never failed to shudder slightly when I first saw from the air that long, jagged barrier of mountains bristling up from the back of the plains. Every year I looked forward to seeing my family, especially my grandmother, to riding my horse, to giving myself up for a while to the lively confusion caused by the unforgivable menagerie my mother had assembled at Willowcroft, the family home in Littleton, near Denver. As surely as a tide to the moon I was always drawn by the country itself, the sweep of sky and prairie, the wilderness of barren mountains. Craig, born in New England, found it hard to appreciate mile after rolling mile of scrub oak and cactus, without a single tree, lake, or ocean to break the distance. But he felt at home at Willowcroft and came with me whenever he could. This summer he couldn't, and I was alone.

This time, too, my grandmother would not be there. Nana had died in January, and I could not imag-

ine Willowcroft without her. She had been for me a
lucent calm in the turbulence of growing up; for my
mother, a check on the confusion she created with her
animals. My pleasure in returning home this year was
mixed with apprehension. I dreaded the silence of
Nana's rooms and the emptiness of her chair on the
front porch. And my mother? I wondered if Cee was
spending her life as hectically as ever. Or had everything changed for her without her own mother, on
whom she so clearly depended in ways she never clearly
expressed?

Nana had lived with the family almost as long as
the family had lived at Willowcroft. We'd moved there
in 1950, following a brief attempt to manage a larger
farm farther south. The pink stone house with its high,
narrow windows, steep eaves, and peaked roof was still
very much as it had been in the 1860s when it was
built, even down to the decorative jigsaw fringe that
was tucked into the apex of each gable. It had once
been the headquarters for a huge ranch that spread
from the small settlement of Littleton near the Platte
River as far as the foothills of the Rockies, twelve miles
west. In the normal course of births, deaths, property
sales, and land divisions, it had dwindled to two fields
and an apple orchard, a main house, and several outbuildings. Behind the house towered twin pine trees,
seedlings when it was built, and in front, shading the
large L-shaped screened porch, was an apple tree and
several young willows which had been planted in 1951
to replace the old trees from which the place derived
its name. Between the house and the front pasture
stretched a quarter acre of lawn where my father, Paul

Wolf, could be seen every Sunday jockeying a miniature tractor back and forth, grasping the wheel as if he
were afraid it would lunge out of control at any minute.

The driveway, bordered by a lilac hedge, led to a
garage occupied by numerous empty cartons and my
brother Bruce's shiny horse show buggy. Bruce was
now in his late twenties, several years younger than I,
and unmarried. He lived sometimes at home, sometimes on his own in nearby Littleton, according to his
current economic status. He never moved very far away,
for Willowcroft, he'd discovered long ago, provided excellent housing for his show horses and equipment. A
few hundred feet to the left of the garage stood a small
red barn surrounded by a large corral, Cee's domain.
On a summer's day she could always be found there,
tramping about in shorts, a manure shovel in her hand
and the inevitable troupe of dogs at her heels. Next to
the barn loomed a huge rectangular two-storied struc-
ture which had once been a part of the main house. In
the twenties, before it had been detached and moved,
it had served as a speakeasy; freestanding later, it became a toy factory. Its final metamorphosis took place
in 1960, when Cee, predictably enough, converted it to
the stable we called simply the Big Building.

When Cee had first seen the place in 1950, she had
scarcely looked inside the house. Her preoccupation
with the outbuildings and the outdoors began immediately and never ended. Nana had come to the rescue
of the deteriorating house a few months later, when
she moved from Denver to Willowcroft. Her maid,
Eolis McGowan, had also been added to the family,
driving out from the city five days a week to attend to
my grandmother's needs. The second floor had been

made into an apartment for Nana, and my parents had set up their own quarters downstairs. While Nana did what she could with the house, Cee cultivated the pastures and Paul tackled the front lawn.

For several years we led what might be called a rural life. We had the illusion that we were practicing life in the country while in fact we were only a mile west of town. Then to the north of us a large farm was sold and a racetrack built, while on the hills to the west expensive ranch-type homes began to appear. Finally the farm directly across the road was subdivided into small lots producing row after row of houses and apartments in addition to the attendant stores and filling stations.

But if the area had undergone a population explosion, it was nothing compared to what had been going on at Willowcroft. The relatively small space did not deter Cee one moment from indulging in her basic instinct, collecting animals. Dogs, cats, cows, goats, horses came to live with us, for which Cee was forced to construct an elaborate network of paddocks, shelters, and pens that would put a city planner to shame. Unfortunately, things kept breaking apart; what the place needed most was a resident carpenter. It was as if the four-legged inhabitants of the surrounding country, squeezed out by human beings, had all come to roost at Willowcroft, whose ten-acre spread was rather grand in comparison to the territory across the road.

While Cee went about her tasks with the dedication of a latter-day Noah, Paul became interested in an animal of his own choosing, the elephant belonging to the Republican Party. Eventually he was elected Arapahoe County Treasurer and was able to persuade the local zoning board to declare his wife an exception and let her keep her suburban barnyard. He looked upon Cee's accumulation with rueful tolerance, for he would have liked her to be free to join him at political gatherings or to entertain his associates now and then.

"Cynthia, it would be a great help if you'd throw a party for some of my friends," pleaded Paul again and again.

"The only thing I can throw is a forkful of hay," moaned Cee after one disastrous attempt at being the perfect hostess. Paul continued with his career and she continued her collecting, and they managed to arrive at a compromise.

Though Cee's activities resulted in some unexpected happenings at Willowcroft, the family underwent the usual changes that occur in most families. My older half brother, David, got married and was now living in Florida with his wife, Marilyn, and their two sons. I grew up, went to college, married Craig, and moved East. Bruce came and went as his fortunes fluctuated. Only Nana seemed to be constant, the still point in the movement all about her. Now she was gone.

The flight to Denver was long. I was unsettled, unable to concentrate on the reading I'd brought to fill the time. As the jet hummed on above cottony plains of clouds, I closed my eyes, thinking of Willowcroft as I'd always known it—the Willowcroft of last summer and so many summers before. Deliberately I transported myself to the first full day I spent there a year ago, when Nana still lived and everything was normal. Gratefully I gave myself over to it, like someone finding shelter out of the rain.

2

Sunrise, Sunset

AT DAWN the walls of the old stone house warm slowly
to dusty rose; horses whinny in the pastures; birds shrill
in the willows. Inside the house there is still a morning hush. Cee and Paul and the dogs curled on their
beds all breathe quietly, while Bruce lies motionless
under a pile of cats on his sleeping porch. Then a
puppy whimpers, a cow moos, and every rooster in the
neighborhood begins to crow. Cee sits up, scattering
animals everywhere. Their day is about to begin.

In a few minutes Cee is dressed and has begun the
routine of care and feeding that will continue in various forms for the next sixteen hours. House animals
come first. Quickly she releases more dogs from boxes
around the room, and to the cats now hanging from
Bruce's screen door she brings cans of fishy gruel. At
least ten dogs have collected in the kitchen, each in its
special place, eagerly waiting for Cee to pass it a heap-
ing pan. Poodles hop, Chihuahuas yip, dachshunds
drool. When their breakfast is served, it is swallowed
whole.

For a few minutes Cee stands watching her congregation.

In her late sixties, Cee is muscular and as brown as leather, her face deeply grooved from sun and cold. In the morning light her eyes appear as gray as her short thick hair. Now they dart from dog to dog in anticipation of piracy. Sure enough, just as several well-cleaned plates begin to skid in stops and starts across the floor, there is a snarl and a scramble, and a red miniature Doberman flees to the community dog bed with a dish clamped in her teeth.

"Minnie, damn you!"

But before Cee can reach her, Minnie the Mooch has emptied the dish in one gulp, accomplishing her first successful raid and second breakfast of the day. Cee runs the whole yapping pack through the bedroom into the backyard, not sparing words. With a sigh Paul throws off his covers and shuffles into the bathroom, where he turns on the radio with a loud blast of farm reports. Only Bruce sleeps on, deaf to all voices raised to the sun.

By 6:30 the barn is throbbing with a life of its own. But there is one more thing Cee will do before she leaves the house in the morning: prepare for the next. Methodically she shoves giant cans of dog food through the electric can opener and scoops the livery contents into a dozen alternate tins lined up on the kitchen table. After topping each with dry kibbles she bears them by the armful to the Dog Icebox on the back porch. This was once the regular family refrigerator, until it became clear that the purple logs of frozen horsemeat Cee used to store inside were not only defrosting with the Sunday roast but overwhelming it. So the Dog Icebox was declared a separate entity and consigned to another room, replaced by a new refrigerator for the family's use.

Opening the Dog Icebox made most people wish they had never learned to breathe. Among the plates of animal food were cartons of sour cottage cheese, meaty old bones, a Christmas box of Roquefort wedges in wine, in addition to several crystallized cartons of ice cream which inhabited the freezer. Nothing was supposed to go in the Dog Icebox that didn't have a tightly closed lid. But even aluminum cans have been known to corrode in this atmosphere.

Posted on a cupboard door is a yellow sheet of paper no one has bothered to remove, though it clearly dates back to one of Cee's absences for a horse show or a trail ride, when KP duties were consigned to Paul.

HOUSE ANIMALS

All pans are marked and are on the top shelf of the refrigerator: large dogs, small dogs, cats, puppies.

Gumpy eats by ladder chair, Mickey in dog bed, Herky right next. Britches under table by door to our quarters. Biddy and Patty north end of table, Minnie on your lap. Spots [cat] on chest on porch, Blue [another cat] on window ledge, Sites in Bruce's room, Hazel in bathroom until Bruce moves her back to porch with kittens and sandbox when he gets up.

Sherman [a coatimundi] will remain in cage. Please be sure he has water—fill left-hand pan with Coke bottle. In morning give him a raw egg and Twinkie.

Paul, unless you want to sleep with Mickey and Patty, suggest Patty sleeps with Minnie, and

Mickey with Biddy. Don't forget Britches in the dog run. Amy [a raccoon] gets a Twinkie in the morning. They are in the egg basket.

Cee marks the pans by writing the name of each animal on a slip of paper which she puts on top of the appropriate dish. (Once she used red ink; when Paul belatedly made his way into the Dog Icebox the next morning, he found nothing more informative than moist strips of pink paper stuck to the bottom of every pan in the stack. Law and order went out the window that morning while Minnie set a new record by snatching no less than five full meals in three minutes.)

Paul also has work to do before breakfast. He traipses back and forth across the lawn, a hose in one hand, a transistor radio in the other. His faded blue shorts droop low on his hips and his arms are a bright red, but his legs are the same color as his white shirt, apparently immune to the sun. Frowning, he attacks a tangle of hoses at his feet, drags a sprinkler to a dry spot, then hooks the nozzle to one of four spigots by the lilac hedge. Music tinkles out of the bushes as melodiously he makes his way to the pump house on the other side of the hedge. At last the sprinkler gives a hop and water spirals skyward on the lawn.

Accompanied now by the 7:00 A.M. news, Paul emerges from the hedge dragging a dead branch. He is about to make another deposit on his "squirrel's nest," a growing pile of rubbish behind the garage he threatens to have hauled away each year but never does. As he approaches the pile, a large goat with dangling ears crawls from her parlor under the livestock chute built into the fence. As she kneels in the driveway to nibble at the branch, Paul stops. Then he and the weather report lean over to pat the goat's nubby head.

Crash. The back door—Cee is finally out of the kitchen. Balancing pans of milk, flanked by a Doberman and a shepherd, she strides toward the barn, her eyes on her toes, her shoulders rounded. Behind her waddles the coatimundi, Sherman, tropical cousin to a raccoon. Cleaned and liberated for a romp, he turns abruptly and scurries up the crab-apple tree onto the porch railing surrounding Nana's rooms on the second floor. When she meets Paul in the road, Cee pauses and they stand talking a minute ringed by animals. He gestures toward the house, she nods toward the barn, as if they were trying to articulate the invisible line defining their separate territories, for only in emergencies does Paul travel any farther barnward than his squirrel's nest. Then the goat rears, plunges at a dog, cats rush meowing from the Big Building, a horse trumpets as Cee presses on, caught by urgency. Paul crunches up the driveway, world affairs hanging darkly in the air. My mother walks quickly toward the early sun, dogs and cats trotting behind, and stepping from somewhere out of the green morning shade, a white stallion appears, nickering.

While Paul, who has finished his outdoor activities, is back at the house grooming himself for his job at the county courthouse, his wife is not in the kitchen fixing his toast and bacon. Instead she is tramping about the barnyard trying to quell the rumble of innumerable empty bellies, a situation that announced itself well before dawn in a rising chorus of whimpers, whinnies, meows, moos, and bleats. After she has slipped the barn cats their milk, Cee fills a large bucket with grain, which she carries with her from stall to stall, dipping out oats by the coffee canful. She gives the mares outside in the large corral their share, then serves the two white Arabian stallions in the privacy of their "houses," which they also use for shelters and bathrooms. In winter, they all receive hay; in summer, they are sent out to pasture.

Rotating the animals from field to field is necessary to preserve the grass, and Cee has learned to juggle her horses as expertly as Paul juggles his hoses. This morning she herds the mares into the upper half of the four-acre field in back since she is irrigating the lower. Next she shoos the yearlings into the large corral for some exercise and lets two stallions stabled in the Big Building into separate pens, where they amuse themselves by bellowing at the stallions already outside. Three hours later they'll all be rounded up again and locked in place.

Once the horses are out to pasture, the real test of an animal lover takes place: janitorial duty. Exchanging her bucket for a rusty wheelbarrow, Cee pushes it around the corral, shoveling manure from the ground as adroitly as most women scoop eggs from a pan. Her forearms are bronze, as thick and hard as a man's, her socks rolled over the tops of her stained and splitting shoes. After dumping the morning's catch on the well-seasoned pile by the barn, she attacks the stalls, scrapes them dry, spreads them with bushels of wood shavings from a canvas-covered mound at the other end of the barn. The shavings catch in her hair and she breathes heavily, but she refuses to hire help or accept ours. No one could possibly learn her system, she claims. Once in a while a stallion escapes, a foal is caught on the wrong side of the fence, or a mare limps in with a swollen hock. Then the pattern is shattered and Cee forgets about her own breakfast, which may or may not occur about 8:00 A.M.

I make my appearance in the kitchen this morning just as my father emerges from the back room. He is wearing a tan business suit of perfect fit and a wide green tie, and his dark silver hair is combed over the crown of his head in neat waves. He does not look his years. Our greeting is brief; though he has spent an hour and a half dressing, he is in a hurry, and he does not sit down but travels back and forth between the kitchen and his car carrying more papers, another briefcase. Between trips he stops long enough to sip a glass of prune juice or snatch a bite of applesauce from the jar my mother has deposited earlier at his place at the table. He doesn't complain about his morning fare, partly because he can expect a substantial supply of doughnuts and coffee later at the courthouse.

He finally comes to a stop by the sink where he loudly and vigorously whips some gray powder into a glass of milk. The powder, I know, is a substitute for Serutan, a laxative Paul used to take. At one time he would have willingly done a commercial in its name. Faithfully every morning he swallowed his allotted dose until Cee could resist no longer and exchanged alfalfa pellets for the little capsules in the jar. These Paul continued to take for a week, growing more and more expansive about their remedial merits. Breakfast became an exercise in self-control; the minute my father dipped his spoon into the jar, David would cover his whole face with his napkin while Cee jumped up to do the dishes and I studied the ceiling for spiders. Only

Bruce in his high chair seemed to have command of the situation. Eventually the day arrived when we all broke down together, much to Paul's disgust and outrage.

A crescendo of yelps from the dogs in the kitchen greets Cee as she walks toward the back door with a handful of empty tins. In a few minutes she is seated for the first time since she got out of bed, spooning up Raisin Bran and tea with the same purposefulness as she shovels out stalls. Her eye is on the telephone, which has been ringing off and on since 7:30. It rings now. Abandoning the table she moves to the corner of the kitchen and slouches into a chair in a corner between the refrigerator and the wall. With arms folded, receiver pinched to her shoulder, Cee thrusts her legs over a carton of soda bottles and connects with her world.

As she bargains herself into a horse trade, Paul gets into his car and closes the door before remembering the bag of empty aluminum cans, all washed and ready for recycling, that he has parked on the hood. These he returns to the back porch. Then with a decisive roar of the motor he whips out of the driveway just as Eolis, inching carefully over the dog bump, rolls in.

Young, timid, pretty, when she was first hired by my grandmother, Eolis has managed to put up with the family long enough to watch Bruce grow up. She has long since become far more than a helper to Nana. When she speaks everybody listens, people and animals alike. Now she enters the kitchen with a flock of small dogs, including her own two which she has brought with her from Denver. Cee's legs are still sticking out from behind the refrigerator.

"Good morning, Mrs. Wolf," says Eolis to the legs. Mrs. Wolf pauses to return the greeting.

"Good morning, Alice," Eolis says to me. "It's good to see you again this summer."

We hug and talk a minute, then Eolis turns her attention to the dogs.

"Oh, Herky, Minnie, how are you?" Toenails are clicking all over the floor. Suddenly Eolis darts toward the stove. "Will you ever!" Retiring in haste is Jerry the Mouse, who had just crawled out of the burner where he lives. In a few hours, while Jerry scrambles frantically for a cool spot, Eolis will coax something delectable from the few parts of the stove still working. For the part of the day she is at Willowcroft the kitchen and the house belong to her, to Cee's relief. Like Paul, Eolis will range no farther barnward than the garage.

Five strong thumps on the kitchen ceiling—Nana's signal. Eolis hurries to the front part of the house; Cee hangs up the phone; I drain my coffee. The screen door squeaks on Bruce's porch; water begins to run in the bathroom. A cat meows but Jerry is nowhere in sight.

The interior of the house is broken into a number of levels and rooms with two distinct areas: the front and the back. Cee, Paul, Bruce, and most of the animals live in the back, where every outside door has a smaller door cut in it for the dogs to use. Cee gave up any pretense of fixing up the back quarters long ago; chairs are covered with towels and rugs have been removed from the floor. The only thing in the bedroom suggesting a feminine touch is a dusty bottle of cologne on Cee's mirrored dressing table, but the walls are brightened by blue, red, and yellow ribbons gleaned from shows and photographs of the three Wolf children riding horses. A dog door opens from the bedroom to the backyard.

The back living room is dominated by a high mahogany desk full of cubbyholes and stamps which Paul has collected, but he prefers to use two card tables set up in the center of the room for his serious paper work, accompanied by the color TV which blinks garishly in front of the only window. Just off the living room is Bruce's porch, built really for the cats, and a bathroom divided into little cubicles, a vestige of Willowcroft's speakeasy days before the Big Building was detached from the house. Cee added custom-made dog cages to the bathroom and two large closets, one filled with Paul's thirty-year accumulation of suits and coats, the other crammed with her riding clothes and the special costumes—sequined robes and glossy pantaloons—that she wears when horse show classes require both horse and rider to be Arabian. In Paul's closet a light burns permanently if unintentionally. Next to the rusty shower stall is another dog door leading to an outside run.

The front part of the house contrasts markedly with the back, for Nana's influence is strong there and she sees that the main living room and dining room are kept in their proper elegant order—which means keeping her daughter's animals out. The tall clock, high desk, the Queen Anne-cum-Victoria chairs assembled in the long, narrow living room were all collected by Nana. At the southwest corner of this room a bay window under which Craig and I were married lets in the afternoon light, which spills through stained-glass panes above a small tiled fireplace, pooling upon the pink and blue-green rug. At the other end a cluster of gilded grapes glows from the top of a huge framed mirror, and from the top of the grand piano several horse show trophies glint. A photo portrait of Cee in hunt clothes and one of me in a netted prom dress smile anachronistically from the rose-colored walls upon the artifacts of another era; yet seldom, except on Christmas morning, is the family there to smile back.

High and bright as it is, the front living room is about as conducive to sociability as my parents' living room. It is inhabited primarily by Bruce, who has lately discovered its acoustical advantages as he lies earphoned on the rug each evening, listening to his stereo bleat and thump among the antiques. Across the hall the dining room, rich with Hepplewhite sideboards, silver tea services, and gold-framed hunting prints, is similarly avoided. For everyone in the family except Nana, the real living room at Willowcroft is the kitchen.

The kitchen is a microcosm of the house itself, full of contrasts and transitions. Old coats used for chores, gloves stiff with dirt, are piled high on the radiator above the dilapidated dog bed; a fifty-pound sack of Purina Chow leans lumpily against the chest of drawers by the back door. Bridles dangle from the top of the door. Sharing space with a brigade of empty milk cartons by the sink is Cee's nondiminishing stack of dog tins. Breadboxes full of stale cookies and sweet rolls for the "wild animals" line the counters. Anyone wanting to descend to the basement must do so at his own risk, for he is likely to be stabbed by a kitchen knife dropping from its barely magnetized rack on the back of the basement door.

In the middle of the kitchen is a yellow Formica table surrounded by five worn chairs, while a sixth remains permanently in Cee's telephone corner. To find space at the table is a matter of strategy, for it is heaped with magazines, market lists, and bills plus a radio forever switched on and a toaster which sends up smoke signals. Yet in spite of its used appearance, the kitchen does have a touch or two of the contemporary about it, a promise of the good life. There's the new refrigerator that replaced the Dog Icebox, a spotless dishwasher employed only during holidays, and a chest of polished silverware that is brought out for lunch, at which Nana presides. A window providing passage for dinner plates and cats opens from the kitchen to the front porch, where we often eat in summer.

Only in weak moments does Nana pass through the kitchen into my parents' quarters, from which she invariably withdraws as quickly as possible. Most of her daylight hours she spends on the front porch in summer or in her sitting room upstairs, seldom venturing up the few remaining steps to the top floor where my old room and the guest room are. Cee and Paul rarely set foot on the third floor unless they are on a specific errand. If it weren't for Eolis, my reversions to childhood sloppiness would go unnoticed. Eolis, however, passes freely back and forth from one level of the house to another, from the dank earth-floored basement to the cavelike quarters in back, from the comfortable shade of the front porch to the sacrosanct compartment which is Nana's bathroom. And at times she even sneaks the vacuum into my room, maneuvers around boots and blue jeans scattered in her path, sucks a pint of moth millers from the window ledge and from under the gauzy folds of the canopy bed.

Now Eolis swings into the dining room and climbs the stairs to Nana's apartment. This morning Nana is seated in her chair by the window among her books, pillows, and the wooden sea gulls she acquired long ago in New England. The sun nests in her powdery hair and lights her faded brown eyes. Her pink robe enfolds her tiny frame like antique velvet; her freckled hands that hold her book are sharply ridged as if waiting for the skin to part and let the skeleton out. Nana has stopped growing old; the cycle is completed; her fragility has the same softness as an infant's. Only her mind and will betray her: a certain stubbornness that demands rationality from life about her, that ensures the authority of experienced intelligence. Her vision, hearing, taste are intact. She laughs as Eolis enters, nodding toward the porch roof where the coatimundi presses his red belly against the screen and nuzzles the latch.

"Tell Shermy he can't come in, not today."

Opening the door, Eolis gathers Sherman in her arms, walks out across the roof, and deposits him in a tree. She then prepares Nana's breakfast, which she serves with linen and porcelain on a turquoise tray. While my grandmother sips her tea, spreads her toast thick with butter, and comments on the *Rocky Mountain News,* Eolis moves about the rooms, talking, dusting, changing the canopy bed, discussing the lunch menu. Their exchange is constant, elliptical, the familiarity of many years. Only Eolis is allowed to serve Nana her breakfast and to enter the sacred precincts of her bedroom; on weekends Nana waits on herself rather than have anyone so boorish as her daughter Cee destroy the sanctity of her morning ritual. Whereas Paul takes almost two hours to dress but seems to be hurried all the time, Nana's pace is truly that of intimate leisure. Not until one o'clock will she be ready to appear in public, when she descends to the front porch to take her place at the head of the long glass table where we lunch in summer.

Cee, in the meantime, has salvaged the remainder of the morning for a short ride. With trained precision she backs the pickup toward the trailer, stopping just as the ball touches the socket, lowers the trailer onto the hitch, and snaps the chains in place. Her horse, already saddled, jumps obligingly into the trailer, and off they bump down the driveway, the mare's rump and tail just visible above the endgate. At one time it was possible to ride on horseback directly from Willowcroft, but since the advent of housing developments, the nearest stretch of open land is a friend's 35,000-acre ranch fifteen miles to the south. Fortunately, all the horses are accustomed to being taken for a ride before giving one.

Today is not, thank God, a shopping day. Thursday Cee will grumble off to the grocery store armed with a blank check and a piece of scratch paper in various scripts compiled by whoever happens to sit at the kitchen table. Her twice-weekly marketing has become a legend; it reflects not only her basic lack of interest in food but in the whole range of domesticity that goes with it. Starting at one end of the store, her grocery cart before her like the cowcatcher on a locomotive, she will speed down one aisle and up the next, snatching items indiscriminately from the shelves, oblivious to brand, quantity, quality, or price. Since fresh fruits and vegetables require selection and weighing, they're ignored. She will stop once to ask for a carton of canned dog food and a loaf of day-old bread for Samantha the kinkajou, but she'll never turn back. In ten minutes she will be fidgeting in the check-out line, her cart topped with Samantha's bread, a lumpy sack of dog chow riding underneath. Crammed somewhere in the middle there will be a frozen cake for herself.

But today she is free to ride, and pickup and trailer are for a moment lost in the dust as Cee zooms out of the driveway onto the road.

Everyone is home for lunch. Thanks to Nana, one o'clock is probably the only hour at Willowcroft rigidly observed; anyone arriving late to the table must fend for himself. It is often easier for Cee to run her horses in from pasture than for Eolis to round up the family at lunchtime, but she manages smoothly today and we file onto the porch one by one. Paul has returned from his office, Cee is back from her ride, Bruce has come from the barn. Nana enters last, leaning on Eolis's arm; she is propped in her seat and pillowed by Cee and chorused hello by the rest of us. Graciously she nods in tribute, small, cool, and immaculate at the head of the table; her blue silk dress and pearl earrings are a mute comment on Cee's old shoes and my knee-worn pants. Nana long ago yielded to the female members of her family and dropped the requirement of a dress at meals, but occasionally she wonders out loud what her daughter and granddaughter would look like in one. Daintily she rings the silver bell by her plate.

"I didn't expect you home today, Paul. You got away so late this morning."

At the other end of the table my father shakes his head while Bruce winks at me. Our father's extended morning departures are not new.

"Are you very busy now with your politics?" Nana asks more kindly as she dips her spoon into a silver bowl of melted cheese held decorously by Eolis in a clean white apron. Paul assures her of the work he has to do, meetings he has to attend, parties he must appear at if he expects to run again for county treasurer in the fall. Bruce and I have a little talk about jazz, an interest we have somewhat in common. For several years Bruce spent his evenings with a local combo playing the drums, an electric-blue set of skins, traps, and pedals now dustily at rest in the corner of the living room. Cee, munching abstractedly, gazes toward the road.

"What is it, Cynthia?" Nana's voice is sharp. Her idea of a family meal is symphonic; she imagines herself conducting a perfect conversational score. But her efforts have always been in vain, though she still struggles gamely against internal discord and outside agitation—the horse buyer who pulls in at 1:05 before Eolis has passed the rolls, the sudden cacophony of the pack of dogs, the phone jangling in the kitchen.

"The vet's supposed to come."

"Oh." No sense arguing about that; the veterinarian takes priority whenever he chooses to arrive.

Cee drags her eyes back to the table. "How's your hip today, Mother?" She watches the old lady's face, trying to read the reaction behind the predictable words.

"Oh, fine, fine."

"You were up three times last night. I heard you."
Cee's gruffness does not hide the concern in her voice,
for Nana's wellbeing is vital to her. She behaves toward
her mother much as she did as a child, willfully disobey-
ing her at times yet invariably governed by her decisions.

"Well, that was nothing." Displeased, almost petu-
lant, Nana reaches for the bell again. In spite of her
history of stroke, coronary, and fractured hip, to admit weak health is to confess a crime. "What were you
doing, listening for me?"

Cee smiles, and her eyes soften in her long face.
Her love for her mother is not unmixed with fear,
the fear of a small girl who turned to animals because
she was afraid of people, of a woman who has placed
the burden of her trust in creatures that uncritically
respond to her. Cee found long ago that bluntness
with human beings was a way of self-protection, eccen-
tricity a kind of refuge. But it is Nana who knows all
the chinks in Cee's rough exterior, just where every
crack begins.

"What's the vet coming for?" demands Bruce, his
bronze face suddenly all attention. I can't help wishing
I had his tan instead of my pallor, but at least his nose
is as red as mine.

"Rouf's flu shot. There's a show next weekend, you
know."

"Listen," Bruce commands in his getting-down-to-
business voice, addressing himself to Cee. "We can put
him in English Pleasure. It's two classes before the driving class, and it'll be good to warm him up. Why don't
you ride Tishka instead?"

"In what?"

"English Pleasure."

"I was going to anyway. She's my horse, after all."

"Mother . . ." Bruce, who had planned to ride Tishka before he thought of Rouf, flops back in his chair, exasperated. "O.K. then. But you've got to help me change clothes between classes."

Nana sighs and relinquishes her baton. "Yes, I will have more tea, thank you." She nods to Eolis, who is peering through the kitchen window. "Are you finished, Paul? Are you, Alice?"

We are both caught with our mouths full of crackers. Nana folds her hands as Cee and Bruce immerse themselves in details of the coming horse show and Paul stabs industriously at his plate. Then the veterinarian sweeps up the road and the two horsemen sweep out the door, leaving the rest of the family abruptly shoaled upon the luncheon table. Nana brightens at once.

"Well, Paul, I'm glad you enjoyed lunch."

"You bet I did, Muddie." Paul's brown eyes are magnified softly through his glasses. When he smiles his face breaks into hundreds of tiny lines, yet his is a young face, squared by a distinctly angled jaw. He has indeed appreciated his lunch, although he can expect a warmed-over version for dinner tomorrow. Tolerant as he is about whatever is put on his plate, he nevertheless almost always manages to get home when Eolis is doing the cooking.

Eolis enters with two silver trays, old gingersnaps on one, old sugar cookies on the other. After a moment's hesitation, I decide the latter are edible, although from long experience I've learned to take inventory of the cookies in the breadbox the day I arrive at Willowcroft, then buy a fresh pack next market day. Cautiously my father and I help ourselves while Nana distributes gingersnaps to the quivering quartet of little dogs under the table, among them the ubiquitous Minnie, who squeezed through Eolis's legs her last time through the kitchen door. I'm looking forward to the afternoon, to the quiet hours on the porch with my grandmother when she rummages with more humor than nostalgia in the expansive attic of her past.

And today, seated in her turquoise chair with her Chihuahua, Herkimer, on her lap, Nana recounts the time she was expelled from an exclusive boarding school near Philadelphia for walking around the second-story ledge at one in the morning in her nightgown. Sometimes she talks of her impulsive, animal-loving father and his passion for fine carriage horses. Sometimes she speaks of her gentle Southern husband, Alexis Foster, whom she met in Denver and with whom she built her estate at nearby Cherry Hills. Three of her four children were born there, Cynthia the youngest.

"And to think I brought your mother up to be a lady." Nana laughs, tapping Herky on the back.

Little did my grandmother realize in the early 1900s that her vision of Cee waltzing around the upper circles of society when she wasn't playing bridge at the club or pouring tea would remain only a vision. Yet she adapted amazingly well to her daughter's metamorphosis from butterfly to horsefly, just as she was able to cope with the whole climactic span of time between the year of her birth and the 1970s. When Nana was an infant, people were still traveling slowly west in covered wagons to those distant frontier towns called Chicago and Denver. In the more recent past she had enjoyed four easy hours aboard a jet from Denver to Boston.

As a matter of fact, Nana accommodated to almost anything that would get her to her destination. Many an afternoon, elegant in pearls and diaphanous lavender, her white head a crown, she could be seen perched on a towel thrown hastily over the hairy seat of the truck as Cee delivered her to the front door of the Denver Country Club. Maybe when she learned to take advantage of a ride, Nana stopped growing old. She could still change her mind, still get a new idea—here was the vitality, the light beneath her skin and eyes and hair. Only the moon landings eluded her. These she watched and shook her head.

Now shadows have fallen from the apple trees on the lawn, encased the porch, sealing it against the sun. A few dark clouds gather over the mountains but fan south toward Castle Rock—no thunderstorms today. I squeak back and forth in the glider at one end of the porch and answer Nana's questions about my husband, for the glider reminds us both of Craig, who has spent many hours in it, reading and gently rocking, his long thin legs propped up on the tile table in front. Yes, he still enjoys his work at the museum; yes, he wanted to come but had a meeting in New York. . . .

"David and Marilyn will be out in August," Nana announces.

For some reason, not by design, my older brother and I seem to pass each other on our visits home; only during an occasional long-planned Christmas holiday does the entire family ever meet. But I know how much

Nana is looking forward to David's gruff teasing and to instructing her great-grandsons in matters of propriety.

A moth miller bumps against the screen and Nana looks up in disgust. "Oh, how I hate them." In a week the whole side of the porch will be a curtain of dusky millers; in another week they'll die, entombed in lamps, drawers, shoes, their papery carcasses raised as late, sometimes, as the following January. Until the millers expire, the house remains in semidarkness to discourage the thick halo of moths which revolves around each light, shedding smoky dust over everything.

There is gold in the midafternoon, stripes of shade across the lawn, sun flaking through the willow leaves and cottonwoods along the road. I watch the grandmother for whom I am named, composed, completed, at rest among her pillows. Because I was the only girl sandwiched between two brothers, I enjoyed special attention; it was Nana who held me as a baby, read to me as a child, taught me manners as an adolescent, and sent me through college. And bound me with something as intangible and inescapable as light. The same thing holds my mother—three generations caught in a subtle web of love and obligation. What happens when Nana dies, I wonder, when the net tears? For the old woman waits patiently in the long afternoons for the death denied her.

Eolis appears, dodging around my father's wicker armchair by the front door. She has traded her uniform for a crisp blue dress she made one evening.

"I'm leaving now; I'll see you in the morning."

As Eolis gathers herself and her dogs into the car, Nana looks after her, a slight shadow on her brow. "I don't know what I'd do without Eolis." Nor does anyone in the family, especially my mother, who has just marched onto the porch.

"Well, Cynthia, what did the vet do? Oh, that dog. . . ."

Cee drops in a chair with Minnie grimacing and clawing at her chest. "Just Rouf's shot."

"Two hours for a shot?"

"Oh, I put the horses in, and a few other things."

"Uh-huh—like talk on the telephone."

"Well, Verna called. And then Peg. And I had to get my ad in for next Sunday."

Nana's face is a lecture. "Well, just as long as you *sell* something, not buy it. Not another animal on the place—you promised."

Cee looks meek and insincere. "Yes, Mother, I know, but that was a month ago." Her history of subterfuge is scarlet; not only does she sneak animals home behind Nana's back, she delights in it. Well aware of her daughter's duplicity, Nana nevertheless continues to fret about the extra work Cee must do and the risks she takes. Periodically she elicits reluctant promises of reform, especially when I'm around to back her up. But it's a sham, and all three of us know it. My mother lives to collect livestock as some people live to collect the daily double.

Cee nods, heavy lidded, lost to Nana's ironic gaze. It is almost time for chores again. Refusing offers of help, Nana fumbles painfully from her chair and slowly makes her way to the bottom of the stairs where she at last allows her daughter to take her arm. "Now be careful," she warns, "I don't want to fall on you." Cee, who thinks nothing of dragging a hundred-pound sack of grain across the floor, huffs with amusement; Nana must weigh all of ninety pounds. Slowly they toil up the stairs, past the three darkened ancestral portraits hung on the yellow wall. Mother and daughter are almost the same size: one pale, soft; the other brown, hard—both tough. Sun slips down the carpeted steps behind them.

It is four o'clock, and I follow my mother to the barn with the dogs. As Cee opens the gate to the main corral, twelve Arab mares and foals whinny in anticipation, surging through in a flashing stream of gray, chestnut, and bay. Colts duck and scoot around the water trough; there's a squeal, flattened ears, the thud of a hoof on flesh.

"Get out of there, Lu Ann, damn you!"

Last year's pecking order still holds. Lu Ann, Bruce's solidly built half Arab, has been straw boss as long as I can remember. She has the privilege of the first drink; then comes Mariffa, my own white Arab mare, and so on down the line until timid Tishka moves forward, thirsty, ostracized, her big March foal by her side still half clad in its winter wool. A sprinkling of white hairs in its undercoat indicates it will eventually turn as gray as its mother. The mares are now crowding through another gate by the barn and I leap hastily through the fence, but in a few minutes they have sorted themselves into individual stalls and are noisily crunching grain. The system has worked well this afternoon: not a colt caught on the other side of the fence; not one mare in the wrong stall to displace its rightful occupant and create confusion absolute.

"Alice, get the phone, will you." With an armful of prickly alfalfa, Cee heads toward one end of the barn while I run for the telephone ringing at the other. I always have to recondition myself to the number of phone calls that go in and out of Willowcroft, some of them concerning horses for sale but most of them involving my mother's friends, who consider it their prerogative to request a daily disclosure of her activities. These lengthy conversations are so full of proper names, usually belonging to animals, and private references that I feel as if I'm listening to a foreign language. Cee's friends, having survived their first blunt introduction, form a careful circle about her, sensing her need for the security of human relationships, admitted or not. Many a call has she given them day and night for help in nursing a sick horse or delivering a foal or simply for consolation when an animal has died.

While my mother talks I embark on my designated chore for the afternoon, measuring grain. Since every dusty sack in the feed room contains a potential mouse, I kick it gingerly before dipping in my coffee can. Each horse seems to get a different dinner: one gets two cans of oats and one of sweet feed, while another gets all oats, and still another receives a dozen cans of concentrated hay pellets. Each nursing mare must have a pinch of B_{12} vitamin supplement and every working horse a spoonful of liver solution. As I stand among an array of dented buckets, squinting at the instructions Cee has scrawled out for me, I am suddenly joined by the goat, who plunges up to her shoulders in a sack of oats. Mice fly everywhere. The goat and I exit at once.

It is cool in the big barn. The flies, which won't begin to bite hard until August, drone toward the high ceiling, a few stuck like raisins on strips of yellow paper; the mares have thrust their heads over the stalls waiting to get out again. Through the door I can see Bruce driv-

ing the gray stud Rouf around and around the ring behind the red barn, at every turn spraying dust over a
heap of bent pipes in the center. The pipes were once an
object supposed to revolutionize the exercise paddock, a
mechanical walk-trotter designed to lead six horses at a
time, but it was smashed by the first horse that protested
being shifted from first to second gear. It now hunches
in the middle of the ring like a huge, decrepit daddy
longlegs.

In the next corral seven yearlings, all last spring's
unsold crop, munch placidly on their hay. Beside the
yearlings' corral is a small pink "tenant" house which
we rented out the first years we lived at Willowcroft but
which is now used to store furniture and other items.
Behind the house is a small pen where a white stallion
rests on three legs beside the bathtub he drinks from.
Not until the moon rises will the hoary old stud begin to
pace the fence, calling for his mythical herd of mares,
arranging duels with another stallion in the pen across
the way. Finally he'll retire to his specially built house
for a few hours' sleep.

I'm more successful with the goat than the grain,
and I manage to catch her and drag her by the collar
into her stall before returning to the house. I know my
mother will linger in the barn as long as possible, talking, putting out feed, sweeping the aisle, filling water
buckets, showing visitors around, arguing with Bruce.
What finally draws her houseward is not dinner, still
solidly frozen, but the problem of feeding the wild animals before it gets dark and they get lively. To the raccoon and kinkajou curled together in their barrel she'll
bring sweet rolls and cherries; to the drowsy fox, a

hamburger; to the coatimundi, an orange-juice cocktail. Then, if there's no irrigating to do, she'll shower, grit her teeth, and confront the kitchen. Nowhere is Cee further from home.

My father's car is once more in the driveway and Paul himself ensconced in his wicker throne on the porch, a drink and peanuts on the table next to him, the *Denver Post* spread across his lap. His lips form a thoughtful O as he reads. I join him, sip my gin and tonic, glide gently in a lime-green world, rich before dusk. The mountains are clear, lavender, two-dimensional against the lowering sun. Ponies swish mosquitoes in the front pasture and magpies flit and squawk in the cottonwoods along the road to the west of the house. As soon as the sun sets bats will swoop out of the trees and from under the eaves of the house, making low passes over the lawn in search of bugs. Even now the blanket of millers clinging to the screen is beginning to bump and stir.

Or is it my mother in the kitchen at last? I've already put the meat and vegetables in the oven, but with Bruce still working horses, dinner might be anywhere between 7:00 and 9:00 P.M. On my way to refill my glass from the tray of ice cubes perched on the dish rack, I catch Cee behind the refrigerator with the phone to her ear and make a face at her. My mother's cooking, or distaste for it, is well known. The last time Cee tried out her culinary art was at her first meeting with her future daughter-in-law, Marilyn, when she went to the trouble of whipping up a cake from a mix. On went the frosting as soon as the cake came out of the oven; down it sank at once among the cracks and crevasses. Cee took a calculating look at Marilyn and passed off her confection as an English pudding. Marilyn laughed, ate, married David. From then on every failed cake was known as a "Cee cake."

There have been other catastrophes in the kitchen —like the canned biscuits left on the counter that exploded all over the ceiling in the middle of the night, or Bruce's welcome-home-from-college steak which slithered off the broiler and down the entire length of the floor, well carpeted with dog hairs. As for the pork chops Cee prepares when she must, Bruce has labeled them according to the degree of interruption: "shower chops" (slightly singed), "telephone chops" (richly charcoaled), "going to the barn chops" (burnt black).

This evening there is a muffled eruption in the oven; then the door flies open, banging Minnie squarely on the head as she roots greedily under the stove. "Serves the little glutton right," laughs Paul, who has entered in time to witness the event. Cee, however, takes the whole thing personally. "This can only happen to me," she mumbles, peering at the remains of a baked potato hanging in tatters from the wire racks.

Once dinner is on the table, dispatching it is anything but slow. While Paul pokes his spinach and prods his meat, Cee and Bruce clean their plates, noticeably devoid of greenery. In a minute Cee is at the sink, her silverware rinsed, her plate on the floor scoured by the dogs. Paul, intent on rearranging his fare, pays no attention as she hovers impatiently over the table, but I make the mistake of setting down my fork. Immediately it is snatched away.

"Wait a minute, for Pete's sake, I'm not done." But

Cee ignores my protest, zeroes in on Paul, who is even less done, commits his meal to the floor, and opens the refrigerator, where she rummages purposefully. Cake, of course. Over dessert Cee lingers, cutting herself one loving slice after another, until the phone rings. This time Bruce gets to it first and disappears into the front hall for long-winded privacy. Calling her dogs to her, Cee prepares for the one last ritual of the evening, a visit to Nana, who has not eaten dinner with the family for as long as I can remember.

Cee can hardly keep her eyes from closing as she falls into the comfortable chair in Nana's room, Minnie the Mooch linked like a red sausage across her chest. Nana puts down her book and props her chin in the angle of her thumb and forefinger. She looks pale and a little drawn. For both of them the day is over as the light fades behind the mountains. Now the rest of the house dogs come panting upstairs to receive their nightly ration of milk biscuits kept on Nana's shelf. On the rare nights when Cee is away, Paul or whoever is home sees that the biscuits are distributed on time, but the dogs don't go willingly to sleep. Instead they prefer to sit downstairs and howl—the shrill yip of little dogs, the bay of dachshunds, the wail of poodles, all joined in a mournful hymn of loss. Many a night I've flung myself downstairs in my pajamas to add my own voice to the din.

"Good night, Mother."

"Good night, dear. Get some rest."

"Good night, Nana. See you in the morning."

"Good night, Alice. It's nice having you home again."

For a moment the three of us pause on the landing; then Nana smiles and closes her door and I go upstairs, Cee, down.

"Do you want to ride tomorrow?" she calls from the hall.

"Sure." I always want to ride tomorrow. But I know my mother has sixty-four animals to feed before breakfast, and a ride will be time bracketed off, a small space in a crowded, fenced-in day.

Tonight there's no reading in bed. The millers have arrived in droves, crawling over the curtain and canopy, attempting suicide at the light. Behind my pillow a faint buzzing and knocking in the hole where the stovepipe used to go—and I am reminded of another summer, when I discovered to my horror that a mere thickness of wallpaper separated my head from a hive of wild bees in the chimney. Outside a full moon, light seeping through the long windows and across the ledge. A colt whinnies in the distance and is answered by its mother, uneasy with the moon. The wild animals bang and clatter in their cages, the raccoon and kinkajou suddenly engaged in a piercing argument. Then everything is quiet.

3

Backtracking

IF MY MOTHER was born under any star, it was probably the dog star in the year of the horse. As a child she played with puppies when other little girls played with dolls; as an adult she played with horses while her contemporaries played bridge. On one of Nana's annual shopping trips to New York, she asked her daughter, then age eight, what she wanted most. "A monkey," Cynthia answered at once. Always true to her promises, Nana made the long journey from New York to Denver in a Pullman not only with a monkey but also with a Pekingese puppy the monkey thought was her baby. Cee adored her new pet. The monkey lived in a special cage in the playroom, took a bath with her, and periodically swiped butter balls from the table, leaving a greasy trail back to its cage.

Had my mother been wealthy, she would have built a stable with twenty-one box stalls (twenty for her horses and one for herself) and a kennel that provided for every known species of dog. If there was a house at all, it would be self-sufficient: it would clean and vacuum itself; meals would be concentrated into pills to be taken three times a day; there would be no parties to give or go to, except those conducted on horseback. Her 500 acres would flourish with grass and fat mares, whose foals each year would caper along miles of clean white fence.

But my mother wasn't rich at all. There was no way to cram twenty-five horses into a five-stall barn; the four scant acres of pasture overflowed with them and dried up; the fences broke down; the house, which only Eolis seemed to be able to hold together, was littered with dogs. The grocery bill paled in the presence of the monthly grain bill. Yet life at Willowcroft progressed, if not with opulence, at least with originality.

It began obscurely but predictably enough with the animal-oriented genes of Cynthia's grandfather, a wealthy businessman who lived in the nineteenth-century boomtown, Chicago. On the edge of the gold fields where fortunes and the economy doubled overnight, Lucius Fisher made his money selling paper bags. Later he built the first skyscraper in Chicago, which still bears his name. He also built a stable for his string of fine driving horses, among them a mare, Kitty Fisher (named after his wife), which proved to be one of the fastest trotting horses in history. A good part of Lucius Fisher's day was spent racing his horses down Michigan Boulevard, where he consistently ignored the speed limit and bought any competing horse that beat him. His collecting instincts were not confined to horses, however. Once he brought home a baby elephant, but Kitty made him take it back.

His oldest daughter, Alice (known to us as Nana), inherited her father's love of animals, although she was more partial to dogs than to horses or elephants. In fact, her experience with horses was, literally, accidental. When she was eighteen, Nana's father presented her with a fine pair of driving horses and a carriage of her own. The first time Nana drove them, they ran away, the footman fell overboard and broke his hip, her mother fell out and broke her arm, and the horses were so irremediably slashed by the tangle of harness around their legs that they had to be shot.

Nana's driving abilities showed little improvement over the years. As a young woman living in Colorado, she would hitch up the white mare and drive some three miles from her country home to the end of the trolley line to fetch her daughter after school. Only because Cynthia enjoyed the drive so much did Nana make the trip each day, for it took her two and a half hours to get there because she let the mare loiter and graze along the road. The return trip, with Cynthia at the lines, took one-half hour. When the floor of the buggy dropped out one day, Nana continued to browse along, collected her daughter as usual at the trolley, and the two walked sedately home inside the floorless frame behind the mare.

A few years before his episode, ironically, it was Nana herself who had provided the life-giving drink to the oats in Cee's soul. Partly because her own relationship with horses was less than harmonious, partly because her daughter was a timid and retiring child, Nana figured that a pony in the family would be a challenge to them both. She was right. Out she sailed to buy the prettiest one she could find, a high-stepping hackney, the lead in a tandem. How many times the pony had felt weight on his back was his seller's well-kept secret; furthermore, Nana mysteriously failed to observe that the hackney was a stallion. No sooner had little Cynthia climbed gallantly on his back than the pony reared, pitched, and tore through a fence, dragging his would-be passenger by a stirrup behind. For a year after that, the child not only refused to get on a horse, she refused to go near one.

It was not long before Cynthia's stubbornness aroused an equally willful streak in her mother. Nana disliked a sissy, and when her daughter's timidity showed no signs of abating, she embarked on a program she was later to claim as the biggest mistake of her life. Cynthia would ride again or hell would freeze over. The more that punishments were threatened and desserts denied, the more hysterical Cynthia became. Finally Nana did what she should have done months before; she exchanged the hackney for another pony, a milk-white Welsh named General Custer. The child approached him slowly, and as he nuzzled her outstretched hand, she smiled. The spring thaw had begun.

It is impossible to estimate Cussie's influence on Cynthia's life. The epitome of the perfect child's pony, he tolerated all of those miserable things ten-year-old children do to ponies, like tail pulling, mane braiding, riding double at any hour. Yet even Cussie was not to be pushed beyond reason. Nana, hearing her daughter and a friend send up loud shrieks of protest one afternoon, flew to the rescue, certain the girls were being attacked, only to find them dancing furiously around the white pony, who was sitting on his haunches in his harness. Cynthia forgot that there was ever a time she refused to ride, and she and Cussie ranged everywhere together over the estate at Cherry Hills. The pony lived long enough to carry her first son, David.

As Cynthia entered her teen-age years, Nana began to have serious doubts about riding as a social grace, and became more and more concerned about a proper introduction to society, for her daughter formed her friendships more easily with animals than with people. Determined to grow an orchid from a horse chestnut, Nana shipped Cynthia off to a fashionable finishing school in New York City.

The school nearly finished Cynthia. Chronically homesick, she finally persuaded Nana to move to New York while she completed her senior year. One of her first acts in celebration of her new freedom as a day student was to sneak downtown New Year's Eve and participate in a Charleston contest. She returned triumphantly bearing first prize, a bottle of gin. Horrified, Nana poured the bottle down the toilet and swore her daughter to secrecy for fear that she would be expelled. Shortly afterward, the headmistress summoned a quaking Cynthia to her office. It was not about the gin, however, but about the hunk of Cussie's mane tied with a pink ribbon discovered under the pillow on Cynthia's recently vacated dormitory bed.

"She must have thought it was some makings of a witches' brew," Cee conjectured.

During her last year, she discovered another diversion: visiting a neighborhood pet store. She soon talked the owner into lending her a dog, an English curly coated retriever, and during her two free hours each day she paraded Tiger up and down Fifth Avenue. Naturally, the dog became a permanent member of the family until he earned a certain fatal distinction by diving into the sea from a cliff in Bermuda. When her period of martyrdom at the finishing school was over, Cynthia returned to Colorado and quite properly "came out."

"And I went right back in again," she once said.

My mother, however, was by no means the social disaster Nana feared she would be. She entertained a respectable number of suitors, and after much romancing she finally married one of them. Shortly after my half-brother, David, was born, the union came to an end. I never knew precisely why, as she never spoke about it to the family, nor did Nana. Her divorce did nothing to help Cee's confidence, but she had Nana to turn to and her dogs and child to console her. It was not long before a handsome young graduate of West Point appeared on the scene. Paul Wolf could play a wicked tune on the piano and fox-trot Cee right off her feet. He was then a captain in the Army Air Corps stationed at Lowry Field in Denver.

In 1934 Cee married him. Paul's total exposure to animals was a half-dozen trips to the zoo, but, being in love, he consented to take his wife's zoo along with his wife and David, who was then two. Not surprisingly, one of my waking memories was of a small black lamb which shared my bottle. Another was of a dog, or rather the death of a dog, which I saw encased in a cardboard carton, being lowered into a hole in the field by our house. I felt a sinking emptiness that was to be repeated many times in my early life. Cee's remedy for loss was practical: it was simply to replace the dead animal with a living one, or two, or three.

While the Nazis were marching through Europe, Cee decided to raise dachshunds. They were a troublesome lot from the beginning, long, low, loud of tongue, and, more often than not, requiring Caesareans every time they gave birth. One day a friend gave Cee a box of fifty baby chicks, which she left outside a few minutes while she answered the telephone. When she returned she discovered her prize dachshund bitch sitting on the lawn licking her chops, surrounded by fluffy yellow carcasses. Since I was too young to know a dead chick from a live one, my mother put me to work gathering corpses from the grass and bushes, which I piled dutifully in the box like a clutch of Easter eggs. Cee finished off two that were wounded by tying them to the exhaust of her car and stepping on the gas. When a vacuum cleaner salesman made the mistake of stopping by, he was presented with the box of bodies and asked please to dispose of them before he could begin his spiel. He was too amazed to protest.

In 1940 we moved to the outskirts of Denver, our first experience with the country. The additional land allowed a greater increase in animals. New acquisitions included a black sheep who liked nothing better than to ride with the family in the wooden station wagon, and a goat who poked holes in the cloth roof of our 1938 Plymouth with her sharp hooves. Then there was Aromatic Arabella, a black and white pig of impeccable cleanliness who roused the neighborhood each morning by jumping on her hut and squealing for her breakfast. Daily Cee would weave her way through the tall rows of sunflowers that bordered our property, seven sheep, three goats, a pig, and the usual dog miscellany tagging at her heels. At each stop Arabella rolled over for her stomach to be scratched.

At this time Cee abandoned the dog breeding business for the pony breeding business. She soon had a tidy little herd known as Story Book Ponies which she partially supported by giving riding lessons to the children of her friends. I was also learning to ride; paralyzed in one leg from a brush with polio, I was strapped howling on the back of a consenting pony and made to trot in endless circles while my mother stood grimly in the center with a whip. However drastic the measure seemed at the time, my paralysis was cured. Later I graduated to a huge white mare called Hortense, who blessed us each year with a strapping mule foal. When I was five I entered my first horse show. Though I didn't win a blue ribbon, the judge gave me a warm pat on the rear and a large, shiny quarter.

My mother began to take the horse show circuit seriously, driving from show to show with a tiny but virile stallion in the back of the station wagon who amused himself at every stoplight by poking his head out of the window and screaming at the startled occupants of the next car. But just as the Story Book Ponies were making a reputation for themselves, disaster struck. All ten ponies broke into the feed room one night and gorged themselves on so much grain that they all died of colic.

In 1941 things were collapsing on the world front as well as on the domestic. The United States was embroiled in World War II and Paul, by then a colonel, was suddenly transferred to Hill Field, Utah, to take over as commanding officer. As difficult as it was for Cee to uproot, she admitted moving was easier without a herd of ponies. The goats, the sheep, and the pig also stayed behind. After serious deliberation, Arabella was presented to a neighbor who raised pigs. Unfortunately, neither Cee nor the neighbor was knowledgeable enough to avert tragedy: later we learned that the tough old sows had hardly taken time to snort at the humanized specimen in their midst before they tore her apart, limb by limb.

With Cee driving (Paul had gone ahead) we set off sadly for Utah in December of 1942, our animal population drastically reduced. Crammed in the station wagon were the makings of a new dynasty, including a dachshund and her four puppies, a kitten, and myself and my brother David. There were two horses in the trailer behind us. The trip across Wyoming was windy, snowy, and dismal, punctuated by children and puppy stops, the latter refusing to wet on anything but newspapers which Cee had to anchor with stones all across the bleak Wyoming plains. At night we parked the horses, still in the trailer, in a hotel garage. Only the kitten seemed to be at ease as she scratched in the box of sand we brought in case we stuck in a drift.

At Hill Field Cee caused something of a minor revolution. A proper officer's wife she was not. When Paul took charge of the base, his wife was automatically elected president of the officers' women's club. No sooner had Cee assumed her post than she delegated her authority to the second lady in command (a major's wife) and set about persuading military personnel to build her a barn from old airplane packing crates. By summer the barn was built, the stalls were filled, and Cee rode every day across the Utah sand dunes accompanied by David and myself. More often than not I was thrown or run home with until in exasperation my mother bribed me with the promise of a gift if I could stick with my pony ten days in a row. It took me exactly one year to earn it.

During our second winter at Hill Field my mother became pregnant and was grounded only a month before my brother Bruce was born in the fall of 1944. She was back in the saddle shortly afterward. By then several officers kept their own horses at the stable; there was the ubiquitous goat wandering around and a pack of dogs which went with us on every ride and lost themselves chasing jackrabbits. Cee had successfully created a popular diversion to the mundane business of making war. Even Paul, who had learned to manage a horse at West Point but whose form lacked a certain discipline, enjoyed going with us from time to time, especially if some of the other officers came along. We rode everywhere, in the mountains among boulders and pine, in the plains among gopher holes and rattlesnakes. In the summer we trailed around to the local fairs so that David could enter his Thoroughbred mare in the jumping classes. The dwindling allotment of gasoline coupons was a reminder that travel was restricted, but other than that, we could have been back home in Colorado. Even the house, one of those unimaginative brick rectangles known as officer's quarters, took on a certain familiar distinction as it filled up with animals.

David and I were not a little responsible for the canine population. Once having discovered the thermal advantages of a fat, sleek dachshund (the four puppies were still with us) under the covers on a winter's night, we refused to be parted from our respective foot warmers. David's great delight was to dress up the old mother dog in Bruce's baby bonnet and lay her on her back in the carriage with only her snout and brown eyes showing. Then off he set around the base to take his charge for an airing—and to see the reactions of well-intentioned wives and Wacs, who, primed with remarks about family resemblance, leaned over the carriage to coo at the colonel's new baby.

In 1946, a year after the war ended, we returned to Colorado. Since we had no house awaiting us in Denver, we lived with Nana, who had been recently widowed, while my parents hunted for a place in the country. They had agreed that our next move would be far enough from the city to avoid all threat of suburban development. Before long we moved onto a 200-acre farm west of Littleton, only to discover, unhappily, the hard work and expense of actual farming. A neighboring farmer was paid to plant and harvest our crops of winter wheat and rye, but problems such as an inadequate water supply, blizzards in winter, and dust storms in summer were never solved. Meanwhile, on our way back and forth from town we could not help admiring a large stone house surrounded by trees and grassy fields, still rural but an easy walk from Littleton. When Willowcroft came up for sale in 1950, it seemed to be, then, the perfect compromise.

4

Spilled Milk

SINCE WILLOWCROFT is located in what is supposed to be "cow country," it was appropriate that my mother should buy a cow immediately upon settling there. Actually, the cow, a six-gallon Guernsey, and her calf were for Paul; Cee provided herself with a half-dozen goats and a milk separator. Milking goats morning and night, she soon developed the grip and forearm of a hammer thrower. Speed was essential, for the object was to fill the pail and strip all extra drops from the teats before the goat consumed her grain and tried to jump off the milking bench. In her hurry Cee sometimes left the pail too close to the goat's nose, in which case the hungry animal polished off her oats with a chaser of her own milk. Most of the time, however, Cee's timing was perfect, and we were blessed with enough goat milk for all our neighbors with dietary problems, as well as for the family, who hated it. Just once, in her enthusiasm, did Cee attempt to make cheese and almost asphyxiated us all.

While I was eager, I could never measure up to my mother's skill in the milking parlor. To her five, I milked one goat in the same amount of time, an "easy milker" at that, with a full, pliable udder and leisurely eating habits. Rosemary would hop on the milking bench, shove her head into the stocks, which I locked, and begin to nibble away at an accelerated rate. Then I would squat on a small green stool, press my forehead firmly against her side, and clench my fingers around her teats. The first four or five squirts were usually dry runs while Rosemary considered whether or not to relinquish her sacred gift. By the time the rich streams began to flow my hands had become cramped claws. Although the mouth of the bucket yawned hungrily, the streams jetted everywhere else, usually on the cat and always on my leg. By then Rosemary had finished her grain and lost all patience, and I was lucky to retrieve my far from overflowing pail without her putting a foot in it. But once in a while I experienced a momentary sense of fulfillment when Rosemary let down her milk at the first pull as I nuzzled against her warm rumbling belly, squirting away with rhythmic certainty, communing silently. By pleasing my mother's animals, I knew I had been admitted to her world. I hoped, then, it would never change.

As for my father's Guernsey, trying to drain her udder seemed to be as futile as letting the gas out of a blimp by pricking it with a pin. Caught up in the enthusiasm of farming, Paul gamely gave it a try. He did not know what every farm boy learns right away, that a cow has no inhibitions about manuring at milking time, especially if she gets bored. Confronted with four spigots, Paul's milking speed was about half my own. The longer he took, the more restless the cow became until finally she humped her back, raised her tail, and my father was forced to grab his pail and run. These interruptions continued morning and night for a week until

Cee, in the better interests of all, banished Paul to the separator and milked the cow herself. Lacking the intimacy of the barn, Paul and the cow never did become good friends. I remember him strolling out to pasture one summer's afternoon casually dressed in shorts, a lead rope draped over his arm, only to see him speedily reappear, his legs flashing scissorlike in the sun, followed at full steam by the Guernsey with lowered head, her tail hoisted across her back like the colors of a man-of-war.

Among the visitors in those days was a loquacious, balding gentleman, Austrian by birth and gourmet by nature, who eventually owned and managed one of the most successful delicatessens in Denver. We first knew Karl Vogel when his specialty was spaghetti casserole, a great boon to my noncooking mother before the advent of frozen dinners. At my father's invitation, Mr. Vogel arrived at Willowcroft one afternoon politely clad in his city clothes. His introduction to the Guernsey's current calf followed in due course. Extending his fingers, he tapped the calf on its curly brow and turned to Paul to address appropriate words of praise, his tie swinging gently just above the calf's nose. A long sticky tongue rolled out, wrapped around the tie in an age-old gesture, and with eyes half closed, the calf settled down to suck. While Mr. Vogel expounded on the delights of country life, my mother and father stared in fascination. Not until he felt a bump at his lapel did our visitor cast a startled glance at the broad wet nose just six inches from his own. Slowly, without a word, Mr. Vogel put his hands to his throat and began to pull up his half-disgorged tie like a ship pulling anchor, until it slapped limply against his fresh white shirt, as shiny and slippery as his famous spaghetti. The next time Paul stopped in at the delicatessen, Karl Vogel chatted enthusiastically about the animals and the farm, but he never called again.

Whether cows provided more for us or we provided more for them was a moot point, and further attempts at dairying simply faded. Cows and goats frequented Willowcroft during the years, but they were merely ornamental and often virgin. When Bruce passed through his cowboy and Indian phase, whatever unlucky bovine that happened to be around served a limited function as a substitute Longhorn or a herd of buffalo. Bruce took particular pleasure in mounting his Appaloosa pony, shaking out his lasso, and pursuing Coffee, a small Jersey, at a hot trot. Many were the loops that sailed emptily into space; long was the ritual of recoiling. But one day as two young girls were looking on, Bruce's loop settled tentatively over Coffee's nobbed brow instead of plopping firmly in the dirt for the tenth time. There was a moment of universal surprise. Then pony, cow, and rider all flew in opposite directions: the first toward the barn, the second toward the farthest fence, and the last straight in the air before he landed on his stomach and was drawn in a dusty wake behind his bucking catch while his audience applauded wildly.

Coffee had actually been intended for a milk cow; Cee had bought her as a calf and raised her tenderly until breeding time. But when she calved late in the year, she produced too much milk for a single offspring. Rather than revert to the milkmaid routine, Cee decided to furnish the cow with a couple of extra children. Unfortunately, the new calves first developed scours (diarrhea), then virus pneumonia, which their foster mother finally caught. The veterinarian shook his head and pronounced that Coffee could not survive three days. Cee was more hopeful, or at least more tenacious, and she persuaded Craig, who was then at Willowcroft waiting for his assignment in the Air Force Reserve, to carry on as Coffee's nurse.

That was in January 1958, before Craig and I were married. I had returned to New England for my senior year in college after spending Christmas with the family, and Craig, who had joined us, stayed on at Willowcroft until he could be transferred to Texas for basic training. Having lived in New York, Craig's knowledge of farm life was even less than Paul's. He was an "Easterner" to us, inclined to be taciturn and academic; he read books while we talked about horses, and he caused my father to defend, not always happily, the various adventures of the GOP. Yet his instincts were true, for he knew the surest way to win the approval of his future mother-in-law was to minister to her cow.

Few patients in intensive care have been so well attended. Two or three times during the crackling cold nights, Craig pulled on boots and jacket and trudged to the barn to rearrange the pile of blankets and center the heat lamp on the ailing Jersey, who stood spraddle-legged, head down, her sides heaving. One night the heat lamp burned a hole in the blankets, and after that Craig and Cee dragged the tottering cow into the feeble winter sunlight every day. Recovery was far from miraculous. As Coffee's nose dropped lower and lower, Cee delayed her morning trek to the barn longer and longer until it was up to Craig to rise first and bravely stride forth to see if his charge was dead or alive. During a bitterly cold day the cow's temperature plum-

meted from 106 degrees to sub 97 degrees, a change
which definitely signaled the end, said the vet. Sadly
Coffee's loyal attendants piled her stall with an extra
layer of straw and prepared to administer the last rites.
It was then that Cee discovered that she'd carefully
inserted the thermometer backward in Coffee's rectum.

In spite of the vet's prediction, the Jersey opened
her streaming brown eyes, belched up her cud, and refused to die. Finally one morning at temperature time
the thermometer disappeared completely, sucked into
dark oblivion. From then on, Coffee's recuperation was
certain and Craig went off to San Antonio better suited
for the medical corps than for defending the ramparts
against a hypothetical military attack. Meanwhile, Cee
was left struggling with one of the largest veterinarian
bills, including antibiotics and transfusions, in the history of Willowcroft.

Yet she wasn't finished with Jerseys or their prog-
eny. Some years later Blossom arrived, adding a proper
pastoral touch as she browsed contentedly with the
ponies in the front pasture. After producing a calf which
Cee, clad only in a bathrobe and slippers, delivered in
the middle of the night by flashlight, Blossom immediately developed Coffee's problem, too much milk. Never
to be intimidated by the lessons of history, Cee introduced a second calf, which ignored Blossom's welcome
butting and was soon sucking noisily beside its foster
sister. Yet the milk continued to overflow. With a sigh
Cee dragged out her little green stool and her pail and
prepared for the inevitable. Blossom would have
none of it. At the first touch she kicked; after five minutes Cee was kicking her back; after an hour Cee had
nearly a quart of milk down the front of her shirt. She

did manage to extract a pint or two which she carefully strained with the intention of freezing the precious colostrum, only to discover when she returned for it that Eolis had tossed it down the kitchen sink.

In desperation Cee sent out an S.O.S. for a third calf. It happened that she had to meet a friend flying in from New York the next day, and when she heard of a calf close to the airport, she picked them both up on the same trip, putting the friend in a flutter of scarves and bags in the front seat, the day-old calf in the back. As Blossom benignly took her newest charge under her udder, Cee thought her problems were solved. By morning all three calves were scouring from having drunk all night. Once more the cure was tedious and so expensive that Cee had to sell the calves to pay the vet's bill. As for Blossom, too productive for her own good at Willowcroft, she was placed with a large family who loved Jersey cows and, better, Jersey cream.

One of the most celebrated of the Willowcroft ruminants never gave a drop of milk in her life. Goat, alias Tote Goat, was famous for her belly. Although she had never been within bleating distance of a buck, she gave the impression of being perpetually pregnant. She was a large bay Nubian with low-hanging ears and sides which flopped like bags of junket. Goat could be found wherever there was food: in the haystack, in the grain room, nibbling geraniums from the window boxes by the porch, or, as on one occasion, browsing on the living room rug.

Goat served a special function as essential as that of reproduction. She was literally the Willowcroft scape-goat. A good percentage of the problems that occurred could be blamed on "that damn goat," for there was plenty of guilt to be seen in the blink of her yellow eyes and the flick of her saucy tail. Running after Goat with a stick relieved us all of frustration. Goat stuck it out, was always around, always underfoot, always ready to "have babies" any minute, or so it seemed to each new visitor to the place. Only when she was in heat did Goat forsake the comforts of house and barn and amble down the driveway and across the busy road to the filling station on the other side. The first time she appeared among the gas pumps the manager asked a neighbor if a goat lived across the street. "Just the two-legged ones" was the prompt reply. Later when Goat showed up in her bewildered condition, whoever was on duty dragged her back across the road and closed the gate to the driveway. Goat succeeded in spending her entire spinsterhood at Willowcroft until one day she simply folded up from old age, her belly sagging under her like a leaky balloon.

The year before Goat's demise she was joined by a companion, a young black pygmy goat which stood no higher than fourteen inches at the shoulder when full grown. Sister Diable followed Goat around like her own mother and nursed her determinedly, adding to the confusion of all those who thought Goat was in a family way. The little goat did everything the big goat did, even growing herself a small black pot as impressive as Goat's own. Then one hot June day she refused her breakfast and by noon was screaming with pain. Cee took one look, loaded her into the back of the car, and rushed to the veterinary clinic. While an assistant spread a white towel on the clinic floor, two vets pulled on rubber gloves, brought out forceps, oxygen, and antibiotics, and within ten minutes delivered a tiny, wet, and very lively kid. Everyone took the blessed event as a matter of course except Cee and Sister Diable, who both appeared to be in a state of shock.

"But how? And when?" asked Cee. "She's just a baby."

Since the only two males in her life were her brother and father, with whom she had lived until she was four months old, it was clearly a case of incest. Happily the kid showed no adverse effects and was soon strong enough to be given the run of the place with its mother. And indeed, the scene was blissfully maternal that summer as the three goats went about their business. Whenever they stopped for a snack, the little black kid dove under its little black mother, who in turn dove under Goat for a dry, but apparently fulfilling, swig.

5

Dog Days

TO HER CREDIT, my mother did not seek employment at the Denver Dumb Friends League; it was thrust upon her. One day she made an unexpected stop at the deteriorating building just outside the city. The place was in deplorable condition, with pens crammed with diseased and starving dogs and cats, and a manager who was pocketing profits from a side business in the puppy trade. Irate, Cee called a member of the board of trustees and within a week found herself the paid head of a save-the-animals crusade. She was to remain at the League for three years until it was fully reformed. Her weakness was apparent from the beginning, however, for every ugly stray doomed to be put out of its misery ended up at Willowcroft. During these days a motley succession of poodles, airedales, pit bulls, shepherds, bloodhounds, boxers, greyhounds, and what have you (as many as fifteen at a time) trod at Cee's heels and worshiped at her feet.

Her daily exposure to the public's ignorance and abuse of their pets did not do much to improve Cee's temper. Often she would return in time for chores with a pounding headache, too tired to talk or eat. Then, just as suddenly as it had begun, her career ended.

65

One day a woman with a hot red face and a limp, panting dog stamped into the office and insisted that someone clean up the trunk of her car where the dog had been sick.

"Why did you put the dog in the trunk in the first place?" demanded Cee. "It's half suffocated to death."

"I couldn't put the dog in front with the baby!" shrieked the woman.

"Then," snapped my mother, "why didn't you put the dog in front and the baby in the trunk?" A week later she handed in her resignation. Her philosophy of animals first, a long time generating, was becoming articulate.

None of the League dogs enjoying themselves at Willowcroft were returned after Cee's resignation. Among them was a fawn-colored English bull that Cee had agreed to keep temporarily for someone else. Queenie stood around like a miniature colossus and snored uproariously every time she fell asleep in the living room chair. In spite of her underslung jaw and squashed-in nose, which made her look like a veteran of the boxing ring, the dog was apparently gentle—she never barked, growled, or showed any signs of hostility as she shuffled along after Cee. But her loyalty to my mother was Queenie's undoing. One afternoon Cee hooked a half-trained pinto pony mare to the breaking cart and, with Bruce at her side and the dogs in her wake, went for a spin down the lane. Although it was only her third time in harness, the pony trotted out smartly, but when she was turned around, she tensed and shied.

"Steady, that's a good girl," cautioned Cee.

The pony relaxed. As she settled into the shafts,

flicking her ears to the words of encouragement, Cee continued to praise her in a low voice. Suddenly there was a snarl like a power mower; the mare squealed, plunged; Bruce flipped off the seat into the ditch, where he was joined almost immediately by Cee as the pony bolted for home. I dashed from the house in time to see a brown and white streak of horseflesh round the corner, the empty cart bouncing behind her, and crash through the gate to the barn. Clinging on her shoulder like a large pale fungus was Queenie.

"Get the dog! Get the dog!" yelled Cee as she leapt into view, followed by a stranger who had jumped from his car when he saw what was coming at him down the road. Behind them ran Bruce, with stricken face and loud sobs. By the time all of us reached the barn, the pony had lost the cart but the dog, who had dropped from her shoulder, was not to be stopped. The more the pony kicked and rolled her attacker in the dust, the more fiercely Queenie charged. It took three people to beat the bulldog from the pony's throat when she finally came to a standstill, too exhausted to fight back. As the pony stood gasping, braced against the fence, a long red gash flowered just above her jugular vein. The pony was never driven again. As for Queenie, her possessive jealousy lost her Cee, who returned her to her owner forthwith and made no further inquiries about her health.

Even before poodles became popular, there were a number of them around Willowcroft. Susie, a black standard free-swinging poodle who was once a League dog, eventually produced a slightly demented daughter christened Galumpy. Neither Susie nor Galumpy were the coddled type; their coats were unclipped and un-kempt, and for most of the year they were walking nests full of leaves, burrs, and wood shavings which they energetically showered all over the kitchen floor. Once a summer they were carted off to the vet's and stripped of their wool. For weeks after that they went about blackly naked, slightly embarrassed but cool. Whereas Ga-lumpy was retiring by nature and seldom ventured three feet beyond the back door, Susie met the world head on, with few inhibitions. So curious was she that she made daily excursions across the road in front of our house and amused herself in the subdevelopment on the other side. Once, while slumming among the garbage cans at a neighboring nursing home, Susie got herself arrested.

Cee was made abruptly aware of Susie's delin-quency when the poodle sauntered up the driveway at seven one morning followed by a young policeman. Hurriedly he explained that the dog was the owner's responsibility and must be penalized for loitering with-out a license. Susie, of course, had made it absolutely clear just who her owner was. Cee listened patiently enough, considering she was in the middle of morning chores. Then the policeman made a rookie's mistake.

"How old are you?" he asked my mother.

"What has that got to do with my dog?"

"Routine, lady," mumbled the man in blue as he began to scratch out a ticket.

"What do you mean routine? Are you arresting me or my dog?"

"You're the owner, lady—you pay the fine. I got to know your age."

Cee pulled herself up to her full five feet two and glared. "My age," she rasped, "has nothing to do with my dog eating garbage. You can stay here all day if you want to—it's none of your damn business."

She stomped into the barn brandishing her manure fork as the policeman watched wordlessly. Then he disappeared for a while. When he returned after an apparent call to headquarters he looked relieved. "You're right," he said, "I didn't have to ask you that question." He smiled slightly. "I thought it was kind of stupid anyhow."

Cee smiled back, slightly, went to the house, and wrote a check for $5.00, Susie's fine. After her brush with the law Susie was permanently incarcerated with her home-loving daughter.

When several saddles were stolen from the barn one night, Cee found another excuse to go to the League, this time for a "watchdog." She returned with a deerlike Doberman whose coat was much too short for sleeping in the barn and whose temper was too sweet to watch anything other than Cee at her ramblings. To keep up appearances she went back to the League for a German shepherd she had seen sitting uncomfortably in a crowded dog run. By the time Cee got there she found that Tanya, as the dog was called, had four puppies to go with her. Cee took the lot home and bedded them down in the barn. Tanya soon became another of Cee's disciples, following her everywhere, staying in the barn only when she was tied up there for the night. She was as sensitive as Lady was sweet, and though she loved nothing better than to accompany my mother on her many rides, she whined and cringed every time Cee

lifted her into the back of the pickup. It was easier to
let her jump in the cab, muddy paws and all.

Not all the congregation of canines at Willowcroft
were former residents of the Dumb Friends League.
Cee had a fetish for miniatures, but while most people
collected china figurines, she collected the living variety. Gradually her assortment of "little dogs" grew;
they were also known as "inside dogs" since they spent
most of their time in the warmest room of the house, the
kitchen. Some of them resembled Chihuahuas to a
greater or lesser degree: they were subject to fits of
trembling; they responded shrilly to a cat or stranger in
their midst like so many four-footed nerve ends. Included in this group were several stunted dachshunds
and the tiny Doberman pinscher, Minnie the Mooch,
who distinguished herself by possessing an appetite
more appropriate to her larger counterpart.

The whole pack seemed to grow old at once. One
year I counted seven of these creatures in their dotage,
gray around their eyes and muzzles, suffering from heart
trouble, tumors, obesity, and lack of bladder control.
Their favorite spot, even in summer, was next to the
chimney under the kitchen table, where they were unintentionally but constantly stepped on during meals.
Two or three, tightly curled and shivering against the
cold, occupied the dog bed in front of the kitchen
radiator during the day. At night they were removed to
Cee's or Paul's respective beds.

Each of these "little dogs" had its own pathetic
history. Biddy, a buff-colored Chihuahua the size of a
guinea pig, was probably the only dog auctioned off at a
horse sale. Cee spotted her crouching in a cardboard

carton and determined to save her even if it meant remaining in debt for the next six months. Biddy, papers, and box brought the sum total of $20.00, only because her owner bid her up. When she was released she was so thin she could hardly walk, and to the end of her life she wobbled about on hind legs that looked like a bent croquet wicket. But if her physical condition was less than perfect, Biddy made up for her defects with a gentle, maternal temperament. Nothing pleased her more than to be placed in an armchair with Bruce's white rats, whereupon she would make a soft nest in the cushion and lie down to nurse her charges. It never seemed to bother her that the rats ignored her motherly gesture and spent their time poking about the chair.

Another of Cee's miniatures, Mickey, had the good fortune to be dognapped. Cee heard one day about a half-starved, very pregnant Chihuahua chained in a yard near Littleton. Apparently the dog was being constantly pestered by the owner's children. Enlisting a friend who helped her spy, Cee waited until the family had left the house; then the two of them swept down like angels of mercy upon the cowering creature staked in the yard. Mickey made it to Willowcroft just in time to go into labor. Her delivery proved more difficult than the kidnapping, however, and was only accomplished by a Caesarean section at which Cee officiated. One lone puppy was the result of Mickey's tribulation, so birdlike and fragile that he lived in a bassinet under the heat lamp and took his meals from an eyedropper. It was four days before Herkimer, Jr., as he was christened, uttered his first cry. He soon became the favorite of the whole family, people and dogs alike, who fussed like a congregation of spinsters over the tiny creature in their care. Herky was living proof that Mickey had been a lady of discrimination, for out of all the possibilities on her block, she had picked the only logical mate—another Chihuahua.

Mickey was not a rover; she and her son spent most of their time contentedly enough in the backyard. One day, however, when the irrigation ditch went suddenly dry, they ventured under the raised gate in the fence and into the wide world. Mickey at once encountered a car which crushed three of her toes, and as she sat pained and confused in the middle of the road, another car passed completely over her. She was rescued by Eolis on her way to work. Cee frantically drove up and down the road searching for Herky's dead body, only to find him, winded and panting, just as frantically trying to dig his way back into the yard. Mickey was fitted with a minisplint at the vet's and confined to quarters in the company of her son. Thus ended their brief, abortive odyssey.

As if there weren't enough animals in the kitchen, Eolis brought her own two dogs to work each day. Upstairs, Nana kept two to warm her lap, where all was tranquil until one of the kitchen dogs appeared on the scene. Having harmoniously balanced a dachshund on her stomach and a terrier on her knee for hours, Nana only needed Minnie the Mooch to rush upstairs with Cee to find herself with a lapful of fury. Sometimes Nana's dogs would defend their territory against the intruder with a volley of barks and snarls; but often they would turn on each other, forcing immediate evacuation of the chair. Nana claimed Minnie was deliberately provocative; indeed there was a devilish look to the little red dog as she hopped up and down at Nana's feet, grinning like a court jester. But more was involved than canine rivalry.

For years Nana had exercised her maternal prerogative by forbidding her daughter to bring another animal into the house, and for years her daughter and been obeying in word only. A new dog was put in quarantine until the secret was out and Nana had reluctantly accepted it as another fact of life. Then mother and daughter would often engage in another contest of wills. Placing the new dog in the center of the room, they would simultaneously begin to call it from opposite ends. As the confused animal looked first one way and then the other there was a moment of suspense. But to Nana's chagrin, Cee usually won these duels, causing Nana laughingly to charge her with alienation of affection. In all likelihood the dog's preference for Cee's lap over Nana's was simply a matter of comfort, for with Cee it could dig its toenails into her pants and bury its nose in her shirt which smelled of the barn and strange animals, rather than grapple with sparky satin robes or risk a sneezing fit whenever Nana was too liberal with her talcum.

But if one dog belonged to Nana heart and soul it was Cricket, a black and white toy terrier. When she wasn't fidgeting about the room, Cricket was curled in Nana's lap, the indisputable proprietor of its hills and valleys. Occasionally she skipped over to Cee's more earthy terrain but only for diversion. Incurably playful, Cricket became the instant partner of anyone who tossed a ball to her, and long after her playmate had dropped from exhaustion, Cricket danced about with the ball in her teeth, flipping it in the air and catching it again out of sheer boredom. Cricket danced about at bedtime also or when it was time to go outside. No one could catch her but Nana, who sometimes spent as long as thirty minutes trying to wheedle the little dog out from under the bed or behind a chair.

Unfortunately, Cricket's spirits were as loud as they were high, and her indiscriminate yapping so contagious that she inevitably set the whole house to barking while people clutched their ears and shouted for silence. When Nana was hospitalized for a minor stroke, Cricket perforce remained at Willowcroft, much to the frustration of Cee and Eolis, who spent hours trying to corner the noisemaker. Finally Cee's patience snapped altogether and she packed Cricket off to the veterinarian to be debarked. The results were disastrous. Cricket lived one week after her operation and left Cee feeling like a murderer.

For days Cee cringed beneath her load of guilt, making ingenious excuses for Cricket's absence, not daring to admit the dog was dead. When Nana came home and learned the truth, her stoic silence did nothing to relieve her daughter's remorse. At Christmas that year Cee resorted to her old way of solving a problem by presenting Nana with a small, fluffy Pekingese wearing a large red bow on her collar. Dum Dum's protruding brown eyes rolled skeptically as she was deposited on the slippery surface of Nana's robe; nevertheless, she turned a few times, then settled herself as gingerly as a hen upon its nest. In two minutes she had slid down Nana's knee and trotted over to Cee.

"Thank you, dear, for the thoughtful Christmas gift," said Nana. Then, as she saw her daughter's stricken face, she laughed. "You know they all belong to you."

But a few weeks later Herky came to the rescue by appropriating Nana's lap for himself. He was promoted to the upstairs rooms and Dum Dum went down with Cee.

Cats were as indigenous to Willowcroft as dogs, though occasionally the two species indulged in their traditional enmity. In recent years the three house cats and their sandbox inhabited Bruce's porch. When Bruce was home the cats slept on his face; when he was away they moved in with Cee and Paul, a cozy arrangement, since they had to share the bed with four or five "little dogs." By 4:00 A.M., Willie the Siamese had grown tired of it all and had climbed to the top of the seven-foot bookcase, where he waited, bright-eyed and solitary, for the precise moment to dive gracefully onto Cee's stomach. Sites, a black and white cat of uncertain ancestry, was not inclined to putter around the house at night but preferred to hunt outside in classical feline style. Naturally he had to present his kill at once to the sleeping humans, and many a mouse was offered to my parents in the middle of the night which was not received with the greatest goodwill. Sometimes Sites forwent his little ritual by simply dropping a decapitated squirrel into Paul's slipper where he'd be sure to find it in the morning. Cee once discovered a dead mouse in the toe of her high rubber boot, but whether it died there on its own or was a gift from Sites was never determined. It did not stop her from wearing the boot for chores the rest of the winter, though she had to air out her foot after each use.

The third house cat, Blue, an ancient, crooked-tail Siamese, confined her nocturnal rambles to the kitchen, where she preyed on everything edible except mice. Every night she upset the milk cartons full of scraps by the sink. If they yielded nothing better than shells and skins, she attacked the bread box, jammed her paw in the door until she sprung the latch, and made a meal of cookies and sweet rolls. At one time, her favorite daytime occupation was to sit beside the dog door between the bedroom and the backyard and bat each dog smartly across the face as it scrambled through. Only after the entire population of house dogs took to wetting on the rug rather than brave Blue's claw was the old lady banished to Bruce's porch.

Barn cats came and went; sometimes they disappeared mysteriously but they never died of starvation, for there were enough mice generated in the grain room to keep the cats of Rome supplied. Bruce, whose special interest was in cats, saw that the proper ratio of feline to rodent was maintained. As a little boy he was fascinated by a litter of kittens born in the hayloft and liked to carry them around with him inside his shirt. One day he found a large mayonnaise jar filled with nails; he emptied the nails on the floor of the barn, caught one of the kittens in the loft, gently pushed the kitten inside the jar, and screwed on the lid. For the rest of the day he toted the jar around with him, hiding it sometimes in the hay, talking constantly to the kitten which had long since ceased to scratch at its glass walls and lay rigid with milky eyes and bared teeth. In due time Cee discovered the victim and realized what had happened. Too upset to bother with explanations, she made Bruce bury the kitten himself. It was only then that he understood.

In addition to the regular inhabitants of the back rooms, Cee once harbored a little animal that would, under normal circumstances, have made an excellent meal for either the dogs or the cats parading about. This was Cee's hamster. My own hamsters were upstairs in my room busily propagating in an aquarium filled with cedar chips, but Cee liked to keep hers, a fine fat female named Sugar, on view in her bathroom. Sugar lived in a small wire cage with an exercise wheel badly in need of oil. Every night, all night, she squeaked around and around at a frantic pace. Then one morning when Cee appeared with the usual offering of lettuce leaves, she found the cage door open and the hamster gone. The cats were still asleep with Bruce on the back porch and most of the dogs were shut up, but even if Sugar managed to remain undevoured, chances were she was lost forever in the wilderness of bookshelves, drawers, boxes, and stacks of newspapers that graced my parents' quarters. Cee resigned herself to an empty cage.

That night, however, the silenced wheel kept her awake, and about 1:00 A.M. she heard a sound coming from the inner recesses of the bathroom, a dim but persistent gnawing. Taking her flashlight, Cee crawled along on her hands and knees until she found a small hole between the floor and the wall where the noise seemed loudest. How a well-fed, thick-coated hamster could fit through the hole in the first place was a mystery, but however she got in, she couldn't get out. Cee left long enough to fetch a chisel; then, sitting crosslegged with the flashlight propped against the wall, she went to work. After thirty minutes the gnawing stopped and Cee returned to bed.

"What were you doing?" asked Paul, brushing a dog from his stomach.

"Just tearing down the wall," grumbled Cee.

During the day the hamster slept while my mother, not exactly a night animal, performed her multitudinous chores. The next night about the same time the gnawing began again, and Cee dutifully rose from her bed and took up her flashlight and chisel while Paul slept on in blissful unconcern. For a week the nocturnal rendezvous continued, Cee and Sugar whittling ever closer to one another. At last from the now spacious hole in the wall staggered a skinny rack of the rodent that was, a small Lazarus returned with sunken pouches and matted fur. Cee cupped the hamster in her hands and carried her to the cage, where she was watered and lettuced until she could eat no more. The next night Cee slept from sunset to sunrise while the wheel squeaked on and on and on.

Cee serves breakfast to coatimundi

Big Building, Red Barn, ponies and friend

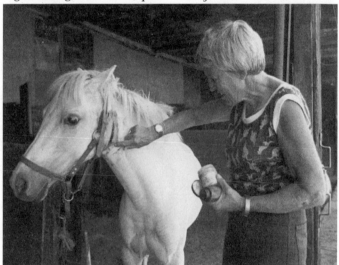

Cee doctors a wound

Chores   *Minnie the Mule, 1987*

A safe perch for the night

Bottom of the Kibbles barrel

The Yellow Submarine

Paul throws a crumb

In from pasture

New purchases, 1987

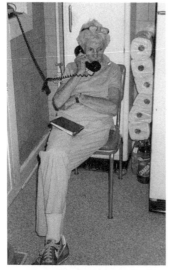

Communicating   *Laundry room denizens*

Miss Piggy, 1988

Middlefield Road development

6

Mares Eat Oats

FROM 1950 when we settled at Willowcroft, dogs, cats, cows, goats, and other animals throve and multiplied, one breed succeeding another, generation passing into generation. But more integral to the life of the place than all these species combined were the horses. From the beginning they held the center ring and determined the activity of each day, the direction of every season. More than any other animal they were the expression of my mother's childhood dream and adult indulgence.

Cee's love for horses may have secured her sense of identity, but she paid a price for it in constant expenses and hard work. There was an emotional price, too. Her passion gave her little time for anything else, including members of her family. Sooner or later we were all frustrated with her, Nana because she did not give luncheons or dine willingly at the country club, her children because she took little interest in our school activities, and Paul because she took even less interest in the politics he was becoming absorbed in, perhaps out of self-defense. Each of us had our idea of what she ought to be, and each wanted her to fit the picture at his or her convenience. If she refused, we were indignant, and the angrier one of us became, the

79

more perverse became Cee, ignoring our demands, escaping to her animals. Dimly we realized that her stubbornness was a form of self-protection; she was timid and unsure of herself away from familiar territory or among strangers, but that didn't do much to avert arguments or alleviate hurt feelings.

Yet Cee's monomania, or selfishness as some people would call it, was offset simply by her inarticulate belief in the people she loved. She would rather run than fight, any time. She forgave everything and we forgave her. Never did we doubt her loyalty to us, if and when she was called upon to demonstrate her loyalty. And there were occasions when Cee acquiesced to our wishes with scarcely a murmur, looking pretty, albeit bored, in a new dress and high heels as we sat around Nana at the club, or trucking her ponies to my school for rides at the annual school fair, or at a party with Paul, both of them laughing as she charmed a circle of people with the latest animal anecdote. Though Nana viewed Cee's activities with both humor and despair, she never gave up trying to reform her. David, Bruce, and I survived our adolescence without lingering psychic scars, and Paul cultivated his own interests. He and Cee spun in two different orbits, parallel yet separate. Their marriage appeared to settle into a lasting compromise.

As with the other animals, Cee's horse collecting began soon after we returned from Utah in 1946. Cee had visions of restoring her prewar herd of Story Book Ponies, which gave her the excuse to pursue a favorite occupation, "messing." Messing meant hunting for ponies to build the herd, first in the classified section of the Sunday paper, then in back lots and tumble-down sheds anywhere within a hundred miles of Littleton. I was a horse-crazy adolescent at the time and loved to accompany my mother on her excursions, during which we felt a great many legs, peered at a multitude of teeth, and debated whether this aged pinto would last long enough to produce another colt or if that little chestnut was really in foal or just fat. If we decided our potential broodmare was a good risk, Cee would make an offer substantially below the asking price. Then, after some hesitations and readjustments with the owner, she would usually walk off with the mare. In the 1950s you could buy a good grade pony for $125, a registered Shetland for $250. It wasn't long before Cee was acquainted with every horse dealer in town and had become an expert horse trader herself.

Bringing a pony home was sometimes more complicated than buying one. If not hopelessly wild, it was often only half broken, and it took a dim view of riding in our rickety, poorly balanced trailer. It would snort, rear, roll its eyes, paw, kick, flip on its side—go anywhere but forward. Cee would then sling a rope under its protesting buttocks and through the slats of the trailer, and bodily drag the pony into the vehicle. If there were two or three people around to help, we would sometimes simply lift the pony into the trailer when it paused to catch its breath. Then off we would drive to the sound of crashing boards and hysterical neighing, especially in the case of newly separated mares and foals.

Some ponies rocked from side to side in their grief, making the trailer weave down the road like a snake in a furrow. Before we learned the finer techniques of hauling we had accidents: a colt, tied by a short rope, threw itself and broke its neck; a mare who jammed her hind legs between the trailer floor and the endgate was discovered only after she had been dragged a mile with severely torn ligaments. Once home, we had to creep under Nana's window hoping that the pony wouldn't choose that moment to whinny. Unloading the animal was no problem; it was only too glad to see the gate go down and to leap with flared nostrils and wide eyes into its new corral.

After a few years of messing, Cee had accumulated a self-perpetuating herd of ponies, half of them registered Shetlands. Each spring more foals arrived, shaggy, stocky, light enough to carry, unbelievably strong. Cee no longer gave riding lessons, but she was not adverse to conducting free seminars in sex education. During the breeding season I would often invite my school friends out for a weekend, and Cee, as a matter of ceremony, would ask each girl, "Do you think your mother would allow you to see a pony bred?" Of course the friend always answered yes, and we would all troop down to the barn to witness the event.

Actually, Cee needed my help, and she knew she couldn't take me without my guest. After stationing my friend circumspectly on the other side of the fence, I would catch the mare to be bred and her foal while my mother caught the stallion, a silver dapple with white mane and tail. Since he was only thirty-eight inches high, I sometimes had to back the taller mares into a ditch in preparation for his grand entrance. Then little Don Juan would round the corner with Cee in tow, preen himself, nuzzle his spouse, nip, kick, squeal, and mount while the foal ran in bewildered circles around its engaged parents and the guest stood at frozen attention. Afterward the guest was presented with a bucket; while I led, she dutifully walked behind the mare, ready to douse her with cold water if she tried to urinate. Since a breeding took place morning and night during a mare's heat period of four days, my friends all had a good idea of the facts of life by the time they left the farm. I suspect that some parents were not only willing but actually relieved to send their daughters to Willowcroft for a spring weekend.

Birth was a different matter; it usually happened in the early morning and was never as conveniently witnessed as a breeding. Before Cee learned how important it was to attend each delivery, which usually meant spending the night with the expectant mother, she ran into trouble. One cold March morning she arrived for chores to find the barn a shambles, bales of hay broken, stall doors off their hinges, and the dirt floor gouged and torn by a young pony mare who was struggling to produce a foal that hadn't turned properly. The foal, dead by now, had to be extracted with chains. Five days later its mother died of a ruptured intestine. The hazards of raising animals were as well known to Cee as the delights, but death was something she never really became accustomed to, especially when it was unnecessary.

As with any enterprise involving horses, the pony business was far from profitable, yet Cee expanded it, for better or for worse, during the early fifties. Horse shows which had previously catered to quarter horses and cowpokes began to open more and more competitive classes to ponies as the fad for them grew. Along with Shetlands, Cee began to raise and exhibit hackneys and harness show ponies (a cross between the former two). This necessitated investing in buggies, harnesses, and other show equipment in addition to the expenses of entry fees and stabling. She was even lured into importing one finely bred animal from the East, for which she paid $1,500. A year later the market broke. Cee's large herd, which continued to munch oats and hay at a prodigious rate, was now worth little more than $50 a head. If there was ever a venture to be written off as a nonprofit organization, it was Willowcroft's Story Book Ponies.

In spite of the fact she was head over heels in debt, Cee was in no hurry to liquidate her stock. Though people continued to dribble into Willowcroft to see her ponies, Cee's reception of possible buyers was less than enthusiastic.

"What do you want?" she'd demand, planting her hands on her hips, her eyes narrow with suspicion. If they were the usual Sunday browsers, she dismissed them abruptly by turning her back on them and marching off to the barn. If they dared to follow her, she allowed them a grudging tour of the premises, but she made it clear she had work to do and they were taking up her time.

"What's the matter with you?" stormed Paul one day after Cee had turned down a good offer for her stallion, Don Juan. "Do you realize how much those ponies are costing? You've been overdrawn for months and you don't even try to make a sale."

"Do you want me to sell my breeding stock?" Cee shrugged in disgust. "Anyway, those people didn't know a damned thing about ponies, let alone a stud. They wanted him for a pet. The first time some kid pulled his tail or yanked his mouth, he'd raise hell. Then they'd come screaming to me wanting their money back. Besides," she added haughtily, "I have a reputation to keep up. I wouldn't think of letting them have him."

"Reputation, horsefeathers," snorted Paul. "If you don't cut down on your animals, I'll have them hauled away in the middle of the night. We simply can't afford them."

Cee's expression changed to one of weary martyrdom. "Oh, all right. I'll run another ad. If you only knew how long it's taken me to build a decent herd."

"I know," said Paul. "Believe me, I know."

A few days later an attractive blond-haired woman and her daughter drove in and asked to see what was for sale. Reluctantly Cee trotted out her merchandise, including a striking little black and white mare named Miss Muffet. When the girl approached the pony slowly, speaking to her in a low voice, Cee began to soften and soon she was enumerating Miss Muffet's virtues as a child's pony. Still, she priced her at $1,000, an outrageous sum considering the market. Cee was relieved when the woman said she'd have to consult her husband. But that night she called back to say they'd take the pony.

Immediately Cee had misgivings. "Where are you going to keep her?" she asked.

"Why, there's a vacancy at the riding academy not far from us. We have a stall reserved."

Cee knew the place; it was expensive, plush, noted for excellent care and the quality of its boarders.

Cee looked around the kitchen to make sure Paul wasn't there. "No," she said. "I can't sell you the mare under those conditions. I don't want her penned up in a box stall the rest of her life. She's worth too much for that."

"Oh, dear, my daughter will be so disappointed. Will you consider taking twelve hundred dollars?"

"Absolutely not."

There was a long silence on the other end of the phone. Then the woman asked, "Will you do me one favor then? Just hold the pony until I see if we can make other arrangements? I'll get in touch with you as soon as I can."

"O.K.," Cee agreed, sure that was the end of it.

After two weeks and no word, Cee was certain she'd shaken Miss Muffet's buyer. Nevertheless, she refrained from advertising the mare. Then one evening the woman and the rest of her family appeared.

"We've come to pay you for the pony," she said with a smile. "We've just bought twenty acres not far from you with a lovely house and barn and a large pasture. I think Miss Muffet will like it there."

Astonished, Cee could do nothing but complete the deal. The next day she delivered the pony to her new home and was delighted to leave her knee deep in grass. "You'll probably want another horse to keep her company," called Cee as she was driving off. Within a year the woman, now Cee's good friend, was on her way to acquiring as much unprofitable livestock as Cee herself.

Failures that they were in a business sense, our ponies were valuable in a different way. Somebody once wrote that every child should have a pony (or a dog) to teach him responsibility, unselfishness, sportsmanship. We may have learned a few of those intangibles from our animals. We also learned what it was like to be tossed in the cactus every other day, to be smacked by a well-placed hoof, or to clash with an equine will as strong and arbitrary as a two-year-old's. I constantly found myself in a love-hate relationship with the animals I "owned," though admittedly I had many good days with them. Little brother Bruce, however, got off to a bad start; his encounters with ponies were similar to Nana's with horses—they usually resulted in disaster.

When Bruce was barely able to walk Cee would park him on the back of a skinny, yellow-toothed pinto named Old Lady, who grazed contentedly beside the barn, apparently oblivious to the commotion on her back, while my mother did chores. Squirm and protest as he did, Bruce was never quite restless enough to leap from his perch. The baby-sitting arrangement went smoothly for weeks, allowing Cee to spend many crucial hours in the barn and corrals. Then one afternoon at chore time Bruce's cries reached a higher pitch than usual. I raced from the house in time to see Old Lady, her passenger still aboard, trotting briskly toward a field of alfalfa surrounded by a single strand of barbed wire. With each stride my brother bounced higher in the air, landing miraculously on one side of the pony's backbone or the other. It was apparent that Old Lady had no intention of stopping for the wire, and Cee, though she was running like a track star, was still a good fifty feet behind. At the point of impact Bruce made a graceful arch over Old Lady's head; then he and the pony plunged deep into the purple blossoms. I could see my mother fishing around in the alfalfa and I held my breath, thoroughly expecting her to come up with Bruce's severed halves. She emerged with her son intact, howling, but suffering nothing more than great fright. Old Lady was immediately discharged from future services.

Since there was nothing else to do with him, it was obvious that Bruce would have to accompany Cee to the barn. Still intrepid, he wandered among the legs of horses, cows, and goats; he toddled through manure piles; he tumbled in the haystack, indifferent to burrs and barbs and the sting of horseflies. His innocent confidence in the benevolence of nature was no magic shield, however; when he sought refuge from the sun one day under the belly of a certain stallion, he was kicked without a moment's hesitation. Once Cee had pulled him up and brushed him off, his whimpers subsided and he went on playing, though he clutched his collarbone now and then. Later the doctor said it was broken. Not three weeks after his shoulder had healed Bruce crawled under another pony and was kicked in the head. It was then that Cee began to have some reservations about her youngest son's common horse sense.

Yet she was determined that any child of hers must be able to master a pony before he mastered a book. David and I had both been riding by six, if more by trial and error than skill; there was no reason why Bruce shouldn't follow the example of his elders. In spite of his earlier misfortunes in the corral, Bruce seemed to be developing into a natural rider. In addition he had a flair for self-exhibition essential to the professional showman, simply described as an ego trip astride.

"Look, Nana, see how well I post," he called to his

grandmother one day as she watched him from her window; then for some reason he dropped his reins. With that his pony trotted back to the barn and sailed over a three-foot fence in her way. After he landed, Bruce chose to neglect his equestrian pursuits for more earthbound sports, such as fishing for crayfish in the nearest irrigation ditch. Cee shrugged him off and let him go his own way. Sooner or later she would win him back again.

My mother knew enough child psychology to realize she could achieve very little by force; rather, she manipulated her children quite effectively through their sense of possession. She gave each of us—even Bruce, who had temporarily absented himself from her sphere of influence—a horse or pony for our own. When we were disobedient she threatened to reclaim our animals. Once in a while she yielded to a good offer or a profitable trade and the next thing we knew our prized possession had mysteriously disappeared in the night, but she was certain to provide a replacement along with many rationalizations. So conditioned were we to wonder what we'd "own" next, we began trading among ourselves when the turnover was slow. Even my father possessed and lost a respectable string of horseflesh during our years at Willowcroft.

"Paul's Horse" was the most useful and salable of Cee's collection, for it doubled as "Something for Guests to Ride" or "Well-Broke Child's Horse." Paul's enthusiasm for a Sunday ride had sagged considerably after leaving Hill Field; he much preferred to spend the morning astride his forty-horse tractor riding back and forth across the lawn. When Cee renewed her membership with the Arapahoe Hunt, Paul joined her, not to chase the fox (or coyote, in this case) over rock and rill but to pass the time with congenial spirits at the hunt breakfasts. Only once a year, when August brought a full moon, did Paul mount "Paul's Horse" and join his wife and members of the hunting staff for an extended evening ride. The rewards were immediate: good company, a good dinner, and many gin and tonics under the Colorado stars. Though my mother's hope of converting my father to her ways was dim indeed, she always kept "Paul's Horse" or its replacement in the corral for quick and easy transportation.

My own series of horses dated back to old white Hortense, whom I rode in my first show at the age of five. During my childhood years in Utah I owned a number of unpredictable ponies from whose backs I was consistently thrown. Though my pride was bruised, the rest of me managed to survive these crashes, and I would pull myself tearfully back into the saddle under my mother's reproving eye. I think I learned to ride at last because it was simply more expedient to stick with the pony than to be stuck in the bushes every outing. By the time we returned to Colorado, I had succumbed completely—I not only rode horses, I drew them, wrote about them, even became one. It was not unusual to see me and a group of friends galloping about with long tails made of string pinned to our pants. When most girls had begun to dream about boys, we still pawed and whinnied in our make-believe stalls, reared high on cliffs against a full moon, rounded up vast herds of imaginary mares. Even Cee began to think I was carrying my obsession a bit far. One day, after I had uttered a particularly long and throaty nicker, she asked abruptly if I was getting a cold. I knew then a certain stage of my life was over.

On my twelfth birthday my mother gave me the pony I was finally to own in spirit as well as in name. "Alice in Wonderland" stood forty-eight inches high, a rusty chestnut, probably of Welsh extraction. Her thick, flaxen mane and tail were long and permanently snarled. Her white-ringed eyes gave her an especially ferocious look every time she laid her ears back, which was often enough. No sooner did she arrive at Willowcroft than she established herself as corral boss. There was something definitely masculine about Alice; she harassed her band of ponies with all the aggressiveness of a stallion, yet she was a match for any female in cunning. No gate or fence could contain her—she simply squeezed through or hopped over. "The ponies are out! The ponies are out!" soon became a familiar cry. Often we awakened in the middle of the night to the clatter of little hooves, just in time to see Alice disappear down the road at a spanking trot, the rest of the bunch pounding at her heels. People were forever bringing to our doorstep stray ponies retrieved from their lawns or tool sheds; once we chased the entire herd around the neighborhood for three days until they came to rest in an orchard five miles up the road, sick and bloated from green apples.

I was never certain just which moves Alice planned and which were accidental. At least once a day she managed to plant her foot squarely on mine and stand unperturbed as I writhed under the greater part of her weight. In spite of her bad barnyard manners, Alice remained at Willowcroft for the rest of her thirty years without being traded off. Under saddle she was appropriately flashy; she would dance, whirl, leap in the air like a Lippizaner, yet would settle into a normal gait at my command. She liked to trot more than anything else and therefore was a natural for harness; it soon became a Sunday sport to hitch Alice to our miniature green and white buckboard and clip smartly down Littleton's Main Street. She had just one vice in harness—she would not stand still. If made to halt, she would rear over backward in the shafts, a decided inconvenience at railroad crossings. Hitching up Alice was like launching a balloon: somebody held her head until the last strap was buckled; then we all jumped for the wagon as off she streaked.

She was also a natural-born jumper. Her approach to an obstacle was determined if unconventional; she would trot up to it as fast as she could, shoot almost vertically into the air, and drop squarely on all fours on the other side. I suffered from a chronically bitten tongue during those days, yet I pushed her up to clearing three feet with me on her back. In no time she had turned her jumping abilities to her own advantage and could be seen sailing ungracefully from one pasture to another whenever it pleased her. Once I saw her clear a high fence, her large belly barely scraping the top rail, only hours before she gave birth to a typically lively stud foal.

In addition to her trotting and jumping skills, Alice was also a decent swimmer. She hated it. Before the land around Bow Mar Lake a few miles to the west of us was consumed by houses, we would canter over clover and prairie dog holes to its edge, strip clothes and saddles, and urge our steeds into deep water. Alice invariably balked and twirled while I, shouting, dug my heels into her woolly sides. Then with a snort of protest she would leap directly out to sea, submerging to her eyeballs. She came out of her dive just as abruptly, always vertically, face toward shore, ears back, teeth bared, while I skidded helplessly on her slippery back, a death grip on her mane. Then suddenly she would sink again, leaving her rider to float above her like a disembodied lily pad until she rose in a great spray, pawing skyward. By that time any pretense of control had disappeared and Alice paddled toward dry land at full steam, blowing and snuffling the whole time. When she reached the shore she shook herself with all the disgust she could muster and sank for a roll in the sand as I rolled beside her, breathless with laughter.

Fortunately for Alice, the summers we took her swimming were few. More and more lots were marked off near the lake and more and more houses built whose owners were not receptive to the idea of our horses polluting their crystal waters. Young as we were, we were aware that people had become a problem, slowly but steadily encroaching on our pleasures with new fences, roads, housing developments. Every time a farm was sold in the area, frame houses with fancy names and filling stations sprang up like midnight mushrooms. Each summer there was more pavement, more gates to open, fewer fields to gallop through. Finally it was no longer safe to ride down the public road; what was once a shaded fifty-acre farm directly across from Willowcroft was now a boxy suburban neighborhood, empty of trees, full of cars and children. In order to ride we had to load our horses in the trailer and drive fifteen miles to open country. Years of prosperity had literally fenced us in.

From the beginning we deplored this loss of land and were determined to take a stand against the tentacles of progress reaching across our countryside. Thus the paving of a road became an insult, and one day a friend and I took revenge by riding our horses around and around in the warm, impressionable asphalt. We did not know that my friend's brother, who lived nearby, was watching from his window. When the sheriff phoned that night to summon us to jail, we admitted our guilt and apologized fearfully, not learning until later it was the brother on the telephone. It gave us some satisfaction to see the steam roller return to work, but when it was gone the road was as smooth and relentless as ever—not a hoofprint remained of our protest. For that we were truly sorry.

As fast as the countryside disappeared there opened up other ways in which to indulge our obsession with horses. One of these was the annual fair and races held at the Arapahoe County Fairgrounds. To her long list of talents Alice added a vaulting start and a 400-yard dash that was a match for any horse or pony in the county, and every year I found myself signed up to race. I was scared to death. Alice knew exactly what to expect; she would dance and plunge down the backstretch on the way to the starting line drawn in the dust across the track while I clung to her back, a helpless lump. The ten or fifteen competitors, ponies and kids of all colors and sizes, rapidly caught Alice's mood, and there we'd all be, a churning clot of snorting animals and ashen-faced riders trying to accomplish the impossible feat of standing still for one moment in a straight line.

We were allowed three or four false starts before the official in charge shouted "Go!" Then it was everyone for himself, a dictum we took literally. No manipulating for the rail or conserving one's mount for the final drive; we were off in a mad dash for the finish, shrieking, pounding, kicking, battling to squeeze in front if only to avoid the clods of dirt being tossed from every drumming hoof. From previous experience at the races I had one advantage: I knew that fifty yards before the finish line in the fence surrounding the track there was a gate which for some unknown reason was invariably left open. When we came around the turn into the home stretch I always took a tight hold on my inside rein while, to their jockeys' fury and dismay, three fourths of the field thundered out the gate and out of the race. Alice streaked across the line among the winners, shifting down to a trot only after she was halfway around the backstretch again. The one year that she failed to win, place, or show was when she was facing the other direction at the start.

An event we looked forward to each summer was the Littleton Homecoming Parade. Originally intended to welcome the boys back from the wars, it became an annual festival, highlighted by a long parade of floats, school bands, and riders dressed in various costumes, all competing for prizes. Every year we tried a new guise, sometimes successfully, sometimes not. One year Cee suggested that I and several young friends go as a band of Indians. We spent the whole morning painting our pinto and palomino ponies with sunsets and handprints. We dressed ourselves in long underwear dyed brown, moccasins, black braids made out of crepe paper, and diapers for loin cloths. Since we were short of squaws, we persuaded Cee to join us; she was willing enough as long as she could cover her face with a witch's mask bought from the dime store. Around her shoulders she wrapped a moth-eaten Indian blanket. Then we hopped astride and rode into town, guiding our ponies by nothing more than a single rope tied under the chin, from which dangled a feather. A more renegade bunch you never saw, but the judge was impressed enough to award us first place for the most "original" costumes.

Elated by victory, we trotted homeward into the sunset, our horses responding to their steering strings as if they'd worn them all their lives—that is, until we turned into the Willowcroft driveway, when Cee, in her excitement, dropped her rope. Her horse stepped on it with a jerk of its jaw and promptly protested by humping its back and relieving itself of its burden. Instead of landing as usual on her backside on her head, Cee landed on her moccasins, on the hard gravel road. She swore she'd flattened her feet for life.

Another year Cee and I rounded up as many animals and neighborhood children as possible and went as a circus. What we rigged out of crepe paper, old clothes, dye, and ingenuity might have qualified for a *Saturday Evening Post* cover. Poodles were fitted with ruffs and dachshunds sported hula skirts. A donkey was painted with stripes to make her look like a zebra, and a calf was arrayed in long purple underwear complete with a drop seat that kept falling open. Little girls in ballet costumes perched on the backs of ponies. Then awkwardly we filed down the avenue toward Littleton and the parade, much to the astonishment of unsuspecting motorists.

Along the way we picked up an extra little boy who soberly marched behind the calf, buttoning up its drawers. We were so late in arriving we were placed last in line, directly in front of a real circus which was the main feature that year. Our ponies took one look at the elephants and stood straight on their hind legs, spilling children everywhere. Cee, who was ringmaster, gathered up her scattered crew and requested, none too politely, that the real circus stay two blocks behind. Our ponies continued to dance wildly through the entire parade, their young riders sobbing loudly. Only the calf seemed oblivious to the commotion, and she and her attendant zigzagged up the street receiving much laughter and applause but no prize. As for the rest of us, we were glad enough to get home in one piece that evening, though we felt we might at least have been awarded a badge for marching onward against overwhelming odds.

During my early teens, though I relinquished the pleasures of being a horse, my affection for the animal showed no signs of abating. When I outgrew Alice my mother presented me with a slender bay Thoroughbred jumper. Actright, as she was called, not only had the distinction of being one of the last of the U.S. Army remounts, but she had also been an officer's mare, a colonel's lady. And lady she was; she reminded us of someone's maiden aunt—tidy, well mannered, and barren, with a disposition toward hypochondria—that is, until she whinnied in her low, melodious whisper, the

sexiest sound I've heard from any horse. Actright's one
blemish was an ear that was broken over at the tip,
giving her a permanently quizzical look. She was also
prone to unaccounted-for lameness, especially before a
show, and to painful bouts of colic from which she
eventually died. In spite of her difficulties Actright
taught me what I knew about jumping and won for
me what seemed then a respectable number of ribbons.

My mother actually had no idea what she was doing when she bought me a jumper. Now every horse
show, and there was one almost every weekend, became
a field of competition I was bound to enter. I never
managed to win back more than a quarter of my expenses, which rose or fell according to the quality of
the motel or Actright's health. Her style of jumping was
exactly opposite Alice's. Long and slow of stride, she
barely skimmed each hurdle no matter how high, careful always never to expend her precious energy. Every
time she took a jump she uttered a clearly audible
groan. By the third jump all the spectators were groaning with her, including Cee, who weathered each performance only by keeping her eyes shut. Her anxiety
was justified, for not a season went by without a serious
accident in the show ring—rails split like kindling,
horses somersaulting over their riders, broken heads
and broken limbs. Thanks to Actright's precautions,
she and I remained intact during our three years of
competition. After painstakingly recording pertinent
details on the back of each new ribbon, I hung them
with admitted satisfaction on the fringe surrounding
the top of my canopy bed. Later they were eaten by
Samantha the kinkajou.

Not only did Cee have to chauffeur horse and

daughter to the summer shows but she was drafted as chaperone to my friends as well. She was game enough, and many a night she spent in a cramped motel room, designed for one modest couple, with gaggles of dogs and giggling teen-agers. The dogs and their feeding tins she kept shut in the truck until the motel owner had turned his back and she could sneak them into the room. Her air of conspiracy delighted us; we treated her as someone our own age. Though we had no intention of going to bed at all, we engaged in loud, playful arguments about who would sleep with what dog. They all ended up with Cee anyway.

One time we made her a "pie bed" by taking off the bottom sheet and folding up the top one so that the bed was cut short in the middle. The "filling" consisted of postcards found in the motel desk drawer, hair rollers, and a couple of dachshunds who settled comfortably in the pocket made by the sheet. When a weary Cee pulled down the covers at 9:00 P.M., we suppressed our giggles and waited breathlessly for the expected "Oh, hell!" But she never said a word, just brushed aside the rollers and doubled up her knees. In ten minutes she and the dogs were fast asleep, a lumpy heap curled tightly in the center of the bed.

At 5:00 A.M. she was up again to help hay, water, and groom. By this time most of us were suffering from horse show jitters, and Cee would take over when someone's fingers were trembling too badly to braid a tail. Later she picked up our numbered armbands at the judges' stand and supplied us with Cokes and encouragement between classes. Though a show was nerve-racking, all of us had fun, never becoming so serious about our sport as to endanger friendships. But our escapades tired Cee more than we realized, and she recovered from one show barely in time to encounter the next.

The National Western Stock Show and Rodeo held each January differed from the summer shows—it ran for ten days and was completely professional. Our preparations and anxiety began as early as October. With Stock Show coming three weeks later, Christmas was simply an interruption to be endured. The jumping courses especially required practice; they were not simple posts and rails set around the edge of the ring as in the summer shows but a complicated maze of candy-striped poles, simulated hedges, ditches full of water, and sharp picket fences. Competitors came from all over the West, grimly serious about winning a $50 first prize that hardly paid their entry fee.

None of us did very well; we were happy enough just to complete the course. It was the stimulation and atmosphere that counted. The arena brimming with light, banked rows of faces that disappeared into the haze at the top of the stadium, the four speaking cones that hovered over the center of the ring, vendors selling balloons and pennants, the band blaring "Stars and Stripes Forever," the smell of sawdust, cattle, and manure—this was more exciting than any circus we'd been to. As exhibitors we were integral to it, and our emotions skipped violently from anticipation to relief, exhilaration, and disappointment. Ritualistically we rose before dawn and drove miles in the frigid darkness in order to exercise our horses stabled at the Stock Show grounds; often we stayed until the last class was over at midnight. The possibilities for adventure seemed endless.

Now, looking back, I wonder how my mother made it through those years when I was considering myself the next candidate for the U.S. Olympic Equestrian Team. Every time I entered the ring for a jumping class she would clutch the rail and close her eyes. Later she admitted she was well on her way to an ulcer during that time. Occasionally she would complain about the cost, or the inevitable extra work she had to do to get me off to a show, but she never refused to let me participate in a class, no matter how high the jumps or the risks involved. If my nerve failed, which often it did, it was my fault, not hers. Always, without reservation, she let me have the chance to try.

7

"Just a Few Horses"

HOWEVER INVOLVED she was with my horse show activities during my teens, Cee had not dropped her own interests. She continued to unfreeze her troughs in the winter, deliver her foals in the spring, and collect her animals. During this time Paul confined his chores more and more to the house. David entered the University of Denver. Bruce was still preoccupied with getting around on his own as long as it wasn't on a horse. As Cee's responsibilities began to dictate her life, people asked, "Why don't you cut down and enjoy just a few horses?" Twenty years later they were still asking the same question. The real problem was that Cee kept searching for the perfect horse: something to ride in summer, something to ride in the mountains, something to ride on the hunt—a horse for all seasons. "Paul's Horse" she had discovered over and over again; she had been lucky twice with my horse, but no matter how many times she thought she'd found the answer, her own horse remained a dream. So she kept on looking —and buying.

One of her more unsavory paths of research led her straight to the killers. I went with her one day to the

meat processing plant near the stockyards and came
at once upon a pile of skeletons stacked eight feet high
at the rear of the building, shreds of flesh still clinging
redly to their bones. The smell of blood and rot in
the 90-degree heat was dizzying. The live horses were
packed in small, filthy pens nearby, nosing the few
wisps of musty hay thrown down to keep the breath
in them until it was their turn to be shot in the head
and quartered. They were bought by the pound, both
dead and alive, mostly from sale lots or mustangers,
and were a pathetic bunch of crippled, toothless animals unable to chew, or colts with twisted legs and
open sores. Cee would look them over as objectively
as possible, picking out the few that showed faint signs
of good breeding, and try to imagine them with un-
matted hair and additional flesh on their frames. She
could buy a horse at the killers for less than $50. But
"rescuing" these animals nearly did her in.

There was no history attached to them. They came
by the truckload from nowhere, jammed and sweating
nose to tail, already treated like the hunks of meat they
were doomed to become. A well-formed head or the
spirited way an animal carried itself was enough to
appeal to Cee's sympathies. The first horse she brought
home from the killers was a grass-stained pinto heavy
in foal, so wild no one could touch her. Cee kept her
under close observation in a small corral and waited
for her to go into labor, which she did, happily, in the
middle of the afternoon. The foal, a lively slate-gray
filly, was almost born before its mother relaxed enough
to lie down. The minute she hit the ground Cee jumped
through the fence and slipped a halter on her head.

But the mare remained unapproachable the rest of her life, which ended abruptly when she was struck by lightning as she grazed in the back pasture.

Next came Gorgeous George, a bright bay with Thoroughbred blood in his veins, who had a fit of insanity when he saw the blacksmith. After crashing hog-tied and blindfolded through three fences, George was put up for sale. A mare with signs of Arabian ancestry was very ridable until she started bucking, a talent she demonstrated every time she was shown to a prospective buyer. Still undaunted, Cee plunged ahead with her rescue work, coming home at last with a pure-bred Arab mare, a half-broken chestnut with white-ringed eyes and long easy gaits. Galamba indeed had potential, and Cee was determined to break her. It was nearly the reverse.

Not that the mare was abnormally difficult or wild. There were just some things that didn't make sense to her, like scraps of paper caught on the fence or branches fallen across the path. Instinctively she spooked at these hostile objects. Yet Cee trotted her up and down the road each day, hoping that familiarity would breed, if not contempt, at least indifference.

Several weeks after Galamba's arrival I received a call at school to report at once to the Littleton Clinic. When I got there I found my mother prone on the table, having her scalp sewn back in place. Bit by bit I learned what had happened.

Cee had been trotting Galamba as usual that morning when the mare suddenly whirled and burst out bucking, tossing Cee headfirst in the gravel. In spite of the blood pouring down her face, she got to her feet in time to catch Galamba, and she was attempting to mount when a man stopped his car. Turning white, he suggested he drive her to the nearest hospital. "No, I have to get my horse home first," insisted Cee. Obligingly the motorist installed her in the back seat and crawled toward Willowcroft at two miles an hour while Cee led Galamba through the window with one hand. With the other she staunched her gushing head with a greasy rag she found on the floor. By the time the mare was safely in the barn, Cee's good samaritan felt so ill he could go no farther. Cee asked a gardener whom Nana had temporarily employed to drive her to the clinic. I brought her home several hours later with 150 neat stitches in her scalp, not a bad job for a doctor who had never had a course in tailoring.

My mother was submissive enough that day to go right to bed. The next morning she got up, fed the dogs, cleaned the stalls, and hauled several buckets of water. She admitted that bouncing along in the truck on her way to the grocery store was extremely uncomfortable. After two days of increasing pain in her back, she reluctantly agreed to return to the clinic for x-rays. They revealed a crushed vertebra at the base of her neck. Much to her horror, Cee was banished at once to the hospital, where she was encased in plaster. For six weeks she endured her itchy imprisonment, somewhat less bravely than all her falls from wild horses, and by the time she was released her scalp had healed whitely under her closely cropped hair. Not an hour after she got home she was outside, still in her cast, painting the horse trailer. A neighbor who stopped by with flowers and sympathy was so indignant she left at once, taking her flowers with her. But Cee had decided one thing: Galamba was no longer a candidate for the perfect horse. Cee's excursions to the killers were over at last.

In spite of her setback, however, she continued her search for a suitable riding horse, acquiring and rejecting one possibility after another. This did not necessarily mean selling it. The company in the corral continued to swell beyond reasonable proportions. A good test for each new horse was fall cubbing at a nearby ranch when the mountains were brilliant, the runs short, and enough people were around to pick up the fallen. Cubbing was the preliminary to hunting, an early-morning conditioner for young hounds and green horses. Cee's placid mount, which had stood about on three legs all summer, would blast off like a rocket the minute it saw the hounds, or it would stumble over the first outcropping of rocks it came to, or it would puff and drag so uphill that it would be summarily retired as "Paul's Horse." Occasionally she found a "hunter" with enough potential to be introduced to the regular hunts when they began in late November.

Though the Arapahoe Hunt seemed to be an anachronism on the Colorado prairie, where one might expect to see cowboys driving a herd of cattle rather than pink-coated riders trailing a pack of hounds, it was long established. Founded in the 1920s, it maintained a permanent hunt staff and thirty couple, or sixty, American foxhounds. It differed from its eastern counterparts in that the quarry was a coyote, foxes being rare in Colorado. Unlike a fox, which normally travels in a straight line, the coyote runs in a circle, and sometimes, on a keen morning, hounds and horses swung eight or twelve miles at a gallop. Rarely did the hounds catch up with the coyotes, and never had Cee witnessed a kill. While she may have been dimly aware of the horrifying possibility that the hounds would corner the coyote, she pushed it to the back of her mind. It was as if, like a child, she refused to believe anything could happen unless she was there to see it.

The challenge of riding over the country was the real point of the hunt for Cee. The terrain was extremely rough, filled with rocks and timber, holes, gullies, and thickets of scrub oak almost impossible to break through. During the winter, ice covered the slopes, especially those with a northern exposure, and snow balled up in the horses' hooves, compounding the hazards of slipping. The cold air made the scent keener and the chase even faster. Though danger in moderation stimulated Cee, after hurtling downhill on an over-eager horse once too often, she decided to take it more easily and ride at the rear. There she could avoid passing the Master of the Hunt who led the field of riders, a breach of etiquette not easily forgiven. Also bringing up the rear was a gate boy who opened and closed gates for riders not wishing to jump the panels in the wire fences, and Cee was definitely one of these riders. If her tailbone got sore or her horse misbehaved, which it often did, she could drop back and go home unnoticed. The other reason she did not like to admit: if the hounds got too close to a coyote for comfort, she could turn and run. But there was a disadvantage to trailing the hunt which one day took Cee by surprise.

It was a bright, crackling morning in midwinter and the ground, where it was not covered with snow, was glacier hard and just as slippery. Cee was riding her newest "find," a large, bay Appaloosa mare with a rear end splashed with brown polka dots that stood out as sharply against their white background as the scarlet coats of the huntsmen against the snow. During cubbing Cee's unorthodox mount had advertised the field for miles and had been the brunt of many jokes, since Thoroughbreds of conventional color were the usual horses to appear on a hunt. Cee was unconcerned as long as her mare minded her manners. Always a little intimidated when faced with the formality of a regular hunt, Cee, in black coat and derby, waited as unobtrusively as possible to join the last rider as they walked from the stables where they had gathered. Leading the field of riders was the Master on his chestnut mare. A short distance ahead of him rode the senior huntsman, flanked by two whippers-in, or "whips," whose job it was to see that the hounds stayed together on one scent, or line, and did not wander all over the countryside on the trail of a deer or a rabbit.

From the moment the senior huntsman sang out his traditional command, "Go into cover, me lads, go in and try," Cee knew she was in for a rough ride. With the temperature a short hop from zero, the scent was always keen, and the hounds hit a line at once, stringing out along the narrow trail that zigzagged over the first ridge north of the kennels. Their voices merged with the long, high bugle of the huntsman's horn, challenging the frosty air. The two whippers-in galloped ahead and fanned out on either side in an effort to spot the coyote. As soon as they cleared the top of the ridge, the Master and the rest of the field broke into a run.

After forty minutes of slipping down embankments, leaping snow-filled crevasses, ducking under branches, and catching snowballs in the face, all at breakneck speed, Cee had had enough. Her mare was wet and steaming, obviously out of condition. The coyote seemed to be making a larger loop than usual, which would probably take the riders miles from the kennels and miles to get home again. Cee was confident the hounds would not catch their prey; strong as the scent was, the animal was nowhere in sight. Even if it had been, Cee had often seen coyotes loping easily well ahead of the hounds or just sitting on a hillside watching them run in short, excited circles below, trying to pick up the scent they'd lost. When the hounds and the rest of the field dipped into a valley ahead of her out of sight, Cee decided to turn around.

She had walked about a quarter of a mile and was picking her way through a thicket covering the bottom of a blind draw when she heard the hounds again. Unmistakably they were overtaking her—either the coyote had doubled back or the pack had split, some continuing on the old line, while others broke off on a new one before the whips could turn them. Whatever had happened, Cee was directly in their path, a most serious breach of regulations. Searching frantically for a place to hide before the hounds and whippers-in appeared on the horizon, Cee dug her heels into the sides of her tired mare.

But it was too late; the hounds came streaming down the slope toward the thicket where Cee was. The pack must have split, for the whips were nowhere in sight. As she finally freed herself from the underbrush and cantered over a small rise, Cee saw a half-grown coyote flatten itself against the snow under a bush. Its gray ears were pinned back and its lips were drawn tight in a frozen snarl. Cee jerked her horse around, at bay beside the creature in the bushes.

"No!" she screamed at the swarming hounds. "Stop! Get out of here!" Cee leaped to the ground, beating at the panting hounds with her hands. But they ignored her—only the huntsmen had the authority to call them off, and this they would not do unless the coyote had been killed. Now she heard the blast of the horn as the first whip came over the hill and she struggled into her saddle as the mare whirled, striking out blindly toward the kennels at a dead run. Cee did not try to stop her. She had disappeared before the din of the hounds subsided into the tearing of coyote flesh. When they finally reached the truck, both Cee and the mare were shaking and exhausted. Feeling nauseated, Cee loaded and drove home alone. She never inquired about the kill that day. Nor did she return to hunt again, though she continued to ride at the ranch all seasons of the year.

It was the following spring that Cee finally discovered the horse that corresponded to the one in her imagination, but it wasn't one that she could ride to hunt or ride for every other purpose under the sun. She first laid eyes on Zirra when the filly stepped from a pickup in the early light of dawn, nostrils flared, dark eyes wide with alarm and curiosity. As she stood trembling in the cool air, her tail hoisted like a banner, she seemed small even for a three-year-old. Her back was short and strong, her legs straight and clean. Down her delicately wedged face jagged a narrow strip of white, the only marking to break the fiery red of her body. Her mane, which hung well below her neck, had a tinted quality as if it had been dipped in iodine. Speaking softly, Cee rubbed her hand gently behind the filly's sharp, flickering ears and down the sleek slope of her shoulders and flanks. All the time she felt as if her breath had been snatched away. As with her old pony, General Custer, it was a case of love at first sight.

At that time Zirra did not belong to Cee, nor did she have any expectations of buying her. A registered Arabian, daughter of Witez II, one of the stallions General Patton had brought out of Poland with the Lippizaners, she had been trucked from Texas for sale in Colorado, where the market for Arabs was beginning to grow. Hoping for a fat commission, Cee had agreed to keep the filly until she was sold; now she was willing to go in debt for her. She did so at once. But the $750 she paid for the mare was not unreasonable; in less than fifteen years she would have brought $5,000, so enthusiastically did Colorado horse breeders embrace this exotic strain.

From the moment she set hoof on Willowcroft, Zirra was truly Cee's horse. She exhibited all the hot-blooded traits known to Arabs: she was green and skittish to ride; she carried her head so high it was almost in Cee's lap; when startled, which was often, she whirled in quick circles. Deep in her desert ancestry existed an instinctive hatred for water, and she would snort indignantly and hop stiff-legged in front of every stream or puddle. In spite of her silliness, Zirra was intelligent, and in a few months Cee had trained her to go anywhere without a bridle, responding only to the pressure of her rider's knees. Her walk was fast, her trot long and reaching, her canter rocking. She was as affectionate as she was full of life, preferring Cee's company and sandwich on many a picnic to grazing beside another horse. Cee was even inspired to write airy poems about the little mare which she hid in her bureau drawer under her pajamas.

With Zirra as a start, my mother began seriously to consider breeding Arabian horses. For my fifteenth birthday she bought a young gray Arabian mare named Mariffa from one of the first Arab breeders in Colorado. Since she was blind in one eye due to an early injury, Mariffa was sold to us as a broodmare, but I couldn't stay off her back, even after she slipped on the wet grass and fell flat with me one day.

After her first foal was born, I discovered by accident that Mariffa could jump. When I took her over to acquaint her with a log she'd shied at one day, she leapt over it as if she feared it would bite off all four legs. By the end of the summer, she would jump anything at my signal, clearing an obstacle in a long floating arc before landing with a staccato of crowhops, a habit I learned to expect but never broke. Gradually my concerns shifted from Actright, who kept on groaning loyally but who was feeling her seventeen years, to the younger, more spectacular mare. People told me I was crazy to jump a one-eyed horse. But Mariffa seldom stumbled and even began to win a ribbon or two at the smaller shows.

Until now the Willowcroft animal population had been predominantly female, not only because females were easier to handle but because they were potential producers. But it soon became apparent that Cee would need a purebred Arabian stallion if she wanted to continue in the breeding business. One day she came home from a horse sale with a sorry old stud in the back of her truck, bony, shaggy, but clearly Arabian. As it turned out, Abou was one of the best buys Cee ever made.

She had come upon him by accident as she was browsing around the pens before the sale. Suddenly a ragged white horse in a pen by himself raised his head and bellowed at a passing mare. The shape of his head and the set of his eyes aroused Cee's curiosity; inquiry revealed that he was a registered Arabian that had been trucked in with a bunch of horses from Wyoming, all of them near starvation. Later she found out more about him. Abou had been bred by a top Arabian farm in Illinois, where he'd been the leading herd sire for ten years. At twelve he had been sold to a man in Wyoming for a stock horse, but he'd been abused, and after he had ripped his owner's coat from his back, he had acquired a reputation as a killer. One summer a drought devastated the already barren grasslands, and the following winter Abou and seventeen mares were left to forage for themselves. In the spring the few animals that had survived were shipped to the saleyard to be sold for dog food.

Cee waited as one horse after another was auctioned off. Finally Abou walked into the lighted ring, a young girl on his back. In spite of his protruding ribs and wispy tail full of burrs, he was defiantly alert, screaming challenges at the unresponsive faces staring at him. When the bidding approached $40, the average bid for horsemeat, the auctioneer wearily cited Abou's fine breeding. Then abruptly he raised his gavel and launched into his familiar singsong, "Forty, forty . . . going for forty . . ."

Cee let out a shout.

"Sold to Mrs. Wolf for forty-five." Bang went the hammer. Abou was led away to a prolonged life.

It took Cee almost four years to get the old white stud in shape again. His front teeth had been worn to nubs from grazing on rocky ground, and he'd lost all but a few of his back teeth. With the help of a specially prepared diet of crushed oats and dehydrated hay, picnics on the front lawn or in the neighboring alfalfa field, Abou began to look a little like the Arabian he had been. His neck crested once more, his tail grew out, his ribs disappeared. As for his virility, it was never in question; all the mares that had been at auction with him were in foal (he was then seventeen). The spring after his arrival the Willowcroft mares began producing small Abous, and soon he was servicing outside mares at a stud fee that was twice the price Cee had paid for him. She made the fee higher when she discovered Abou was the grandsire of several national champions. In his roaring twenties he sired some of Willowcroft's best show stock. Fathering happily, Abou spent his autumn years at Willowcroft until he became so crippled with arthritis at twenty-eight that Cee had him put down rather than let him endure another winter.

After the first, stallions were easier for my mother to accumulate. So was trouble. A chestnut named Hanrah, another case of arthritis, made his debut at Willowcroft for the purpose of infusing new blood and color into the breeding stock. Although Abou and Hanrah were easy enough to handle by themselves, the two old boys had to be kept apart, each requiring his own pen, house, and additional labor for Cee. Her justification was that the stud fees charged to outside mares paid for the winter's hay. When a third stallion, Alisan, arrived, Cee was forced to do some fancy maneuvering during chore time lest confrontation take place and a three-way massacre ensue.

Alisan was the result of one of Cee's elaborate horse trades in which she ended up with $2,000 in addition to the stallion. At $200 a breeding, he not only earned his keep but gave Cee the satisfaction of proving her skill as a dealer and her courage as a reformer of so-called "killers." Unlike his venerable elders, Alisan had none of the equanimity of age. Because he slammed his first owner against a fence, he was considered dangerous. When a trainer swore that no man could handle him, much less a woman, Cee could not resist the challenge. Soon Alisan was behaving like a gentleman around women, but he remained suspicious and ill-tempered whenever a man approached him. Nevertheless, Cee managed to train him in dressage and even to exhibit him in the shows, though more in hopes of getting a breeding than a ribbon.

One of the few maxims I remember my mother repeating to me was "Never absolutely trust a horse." While she had no fear of handling an unpredictable stallion and could successfully win its trust, she usually lived by her rule. When she was preoccupied, or tired, or in a hurry, she got hurt. One afternoon on her way home from a horse show with two mares in the trailer she dozed off a moment, and the truck careened off the road, through a fence, and stopped with its front wheels in a creek. Cee jumped out and ran to check her horses, who were standing stoically on their feet after the rough ride they'd just taken. Nothing was damaged, but by the time a man in a Jeep had pulled

Cee's rig back to the road, she was almost two hours late for chores.

The horses were hungry and demanding when she finally got home, and she herself was not in the clearest frame of mind. Alisan was pacing up and down his pen, flinging his head around. When Cee entered with his grain, he plunged his nose in the bucket before Cee could dump it in his feed box.

"Get your face out of there!" Cee whacked the stallion between the ears, forgetting all her months of caution. With a loud snort of surprise, Alisan lunged forward, knocking the bucket and Cee under his feet. Lying in a pile of oats she waited for Alisan's hooves to descend and trample her to pieces, but instead he backed out of her way into a corner of his pen, where he stood snorting with bulging eyes.

Cee was sure her back was broken again. A pony mare was sharing Alisan's pen with him, and when she saw Cee on the ground she came over and snuffled at her. Cee managed to grab the pony by the leg and inch herself to her feet, then stagger to the house. Paul and I were both home but we'd had no reason to be alarmed, as Cee was often late returning from shows, and neither one of us had seen her drive in. When I went to the back of the house for something I heard the dogs pattering and whimpering in Cee's bedroom and I peered in. She was lying on her bed, her knees drawn up, her eyes squeezed shut with pain.

After an endless wait in the hospital emergency room that night, x-rays revealed no broken bones. The doctor was much more interested in Cee's arm, where a large, tumorlike lump had risen as a result of her hitting it on the steering wheel of the truck. Cee figured she must have been in shock ever since the first accident that day, for she only dimly remembers driving home and entering Alisan's pen. The discomfort from the torn ligaments and muscles in her back lasted a year and continued to return with a change in the weather. But Cee was determined to prove that bodily injury was no excuse for a change in her life.

My life, in the meantime, was having its own upheaval. In 1954 I was admitted to an eastern college, which meant that I would be away from home nine months out of every year. It was Nana who had prodded me into applying, and she and Paul were pleased at my acceptance. As usual, my mother had little interest in my academic endeavors. As fall approached and the date of my departure grew near, I became troubled and quiet, for I sensed that the real departure was not from Willowcroft but from my childhood. Late one afternoon when I was helping my mother in the barn, she asked me if I had everything I needed for the trip. My hesitant yes stopped her in the act of sweeping the floor. Leaning on her broom, she watched me a moment.

"Daddy and I will miss you," she said. "But you have to go and you should." Her brow crinkled slightly with the effort to frame her thoughts. "Alice," she said finally, her voice low, "I never want you to feel that I'm trying to hold on to you."

Though her words puzzled me at the time, I felt relieved. But it would be years before I fully understood what my mother had meant, and what a gift she'd given me.

My predictable homesickness that first year in college found its release in much romanticizing about life in the West and, more particularly, life at Willowcroft. Mariffa bore the greatest burden. Cloistered behind ivy walls, I often dreamed of the gray, now white, Arabian I had left in Colorado. She blossomed in my imagination as she had never done in actuality, the epitome of all that was free, poetic, mysterious. I envisioned her always as virginal, racing over fields and mountains with flared nostrils and flagged tail. She was unreflective flight, space, exhilaration—all that I thought was missing in the wooded intellectual density of New England. Though I loved the mare as she was, I nurtured my image of her as if it were the only dream on earth.

One summer's night when I was home on vacation an eerie thing happened. About 3 A.M. I was awakened by a slight rustling below my window. The air was still and the full moon cast deep shadows across the lawn. From behind the lilac hedge drifted a white horse I recognized as Mariffa, along with two other pale-gray mares who had escaped from the corral. Lowering their heads they silently began to graze, bathed all over in the silver light. Then just as suddenly they took alarm at something and softly floated away. I felt as if I had been watching a gathering of phantoms. The image and the reality had strangely coalesced.

My image of Willowcroft and its reality, however, were miles apart. I think it was that summer that I seriously began to count Cee's animals and urge her to give up a few. She looked healthy enough, tan and strong, but most of her day she spent doing endless tasks for her menagerie, taking time out only to sit with Nana or tend to her needs. The long rides that I remembered were short spurts when we could fit them in. My mother's responsibilities had eclipsed her pleasures, and every time she dragged a bale of hay from the feed room or hefted a shovelful of manure onto her wheelbarrow, she revealed how tired she was.

Nana had noticed it too. We were in her sitting room one evening after dinner discussing my college classes when Nana broke off what she was saying and nodded toward Cee, who was stretched out fast asleep in the red chair opposite, a dog on her lap.

"Your mother works too hard."

Apparently we had lost her after the first mention of my psychology and philosophy courses.

"You know," continued Nana, "it's hard to talk to your mother these days. All she's interested in is horses, horses, horses. And all your father is interested in is politics, politics, politics." She eyed Cee critically; then her face softened. "Oh, my, how did I ever produce such a daughter?" She laughed. I laughed with her though I sensed her disappointment and, deeper than that, her loneliness. It was true that Cynthia had not turned into the person whom Nana had envisioned so many years before: urbane, socially conscious, intellectually informed. But Nana had not let her go; she was still Nana's naughty little girl. As I gazed at my grandmother, who was leaning sadly on the arm of her chair, and then at my mother's weather-beaten face relaxed in sleep, I had the uncanny feeling that I was older than both of them. For a brief moment I wondered if Cee was harboring all those animals out of sheer rebelliousness. I was on both their sides yet on no side at all, so entangled we were.

By the 1960s Arabian horses had spread throughout Colorado and in some sections had replaced quarter horses in popularity. As more Arabians were exhibited in shows, a whole cluster of classes sprang up to accommodate them, including something called "Native Costume Class." More a pageant than a display of skill, this class was supposed to approximate an Arabic tribe as it responded to a call to battle. Riders in unbelievably bright regalia lined up outside the ring, then galloped through the gate at a dead run, looking like a flock of great, tropical, flapping birds.

Cee and I decided to enter a costume class one summer when I was home for vacation. Nervously we waited outside the gate, dressed in our very best robes, tassels, and pantaloons. We even wore veils to add to the mystery in our eyes. Then, as the band struck up a stirring rendition of "The Sheik of Araby," we flew into the ring at breakneck speed. After he saw us tilt precariously around the first turn, the judge, who was somewhat cautious, called for a walk. I didn't realize my horse was listening. In two jumps she had downshifted from a full gallop to a full stop, leaving her rider to answer the pull of gravity and sail swanlike over her head before sprawling ignominiously in the dirt. Astounded, I lay there like some glittering green and gold lily pad.

"Why, isn't that little Alice Wolf?" chirped the announcer, who knew me from my jumping days. As I waited for the ring steward to untangle my robes and raise me to a level of dignity, I caught a glimpse of my sympathetic mother at the end of the ring collapsed in a fit of laughter on her horse's neck. That was my first and last attempt at Arabic theatricals, though for years afterward Cee considered the costume class the best part of each show and spent many fond hours selecting a dashing outfit from among the gaudy collection of robes and pants in her closet.

Interest in Arabians in the Denver area continued to expand as rapidly as the city itself until the market was glutted. Since every breeder raised his own stallion now, Cee's small income from service fees slowed to a trickle. Her real market, she discovered, lay in half Arabs, which were less hot-blooded than purebreds and considerably cheaper. One of her best mares was Streak, a flashy red and white cross between an Arabian and a Shetland pony. Like so many others, Streak made her way to Willowcroft via the auction block.

"When I die probably all I'll get is a plaque up over at the North Federal Sales Barn saying what a sucker I was," quipped my mother one time. Her prediction seemed to have a ring of truth the day she bought Streak. So eager was she to own the handsome little mare that she promised $150 for her before the sale began. Streak was billed as a "child's pony," but when she was kicked abruptly into the center of the ring, she stood up straight on her hind legs. The bidding did not go higher than $50. Cee honored her pledge, however, and morosely took the pony home, thinking of all the hay she could have bought with the $100 she'd lost.

Streak soon proved she was worth her price and more. She let anyone ride her anywhere, and once she cheerfully consented to pull the mayor in the green and white buckboard down Littleton's Main Street during the annual parade. Cee neglected to tell the mayor that Streak had never been broken to drive. She began to win everything from pole bending to egg and spoon races at the local gymkhanas, often with Cee aboard. And for better or for worse, it was Streak who finally lured Bruce away from his bicycle and back to four-footed mobility.

At that time Bruce happened to be in love with a girl up the road, and being too lazy to pedal his bike uphill, he found it convenient to hop on Streak's back and canter up to do his courting—not without mishap. His eyes directed elsewhere one day, Bruce rode under his lady's clothesline and pulled a week's laundry down around his ears. Although he eventually lost the girl, his excursions on Streak's warm and willing back rekindled his general interest in horses, a flame that was to grow higher and hotter with the years.

With Bruce as the new horseman of the family, Cee raised and showed successfully a number of half Arabs during the latter part of the 1960s. Like me, Bruce went through an intense period of exhibiting, but Cee wasn't nearly so enthusiastic the second time around, though she dutifully carted his horses from this show to that. As always, she took in more animals than she sold. By 1970 her attempts to justify the cramped corrals and burgeoning barn as a horse breeding business had fizzled out. She was simply a collector at heart. The thought of selling her colts before she had a chance to see how they would turn out was as alien to her as plucking the buds from a plant before they bloomed.

Cee never admitted to how many horses she owned, just as she never publicly admitted her age. The headcount she usually reported hovered in the twenties, though I was aware that each summer before I made my appearance at Willowcroft she "farmed out" or, more accurately, hid a good proportion of her animals with accommodating friends. Suggestions to cut her stock, expenses, and labor went unheeded. One summer I counted thirty-two head on seven acres of pasture, with almost every mare in foal. The yearly intake of grass, grain, and hay was copious enough, not to mention the host of problems that gathered around each horse like flies around its ears. But what could you do with an addict? If there was an organization called Horses Anonymous, I'd never heard of it. Whenever I suggested to my mother that she was crazy to have so many animals, her answer was that she'd be crazy not to. So grudgingly I yielded. If her work exhausted her and her problems overwhelmed her at times, she was willing to pay the price in her own terms, for it was life that involved her and death that dismayed her. The care and rescue and enjoyment of animals, no matter how many, obsessed her—a madness most knowingly embraced.

8

What Do You Do With a Kinkajou?

THE MAJORITY of the animals at Willowcroft were
those which might be found in any normal farmyard.
But as long ago as the sixties Cee's menagerie included
a small but powerful minority group. This began subtly
enough with the introduction of a pair of tame skunks
named Jasper and Minerva. They were, of course, deo-
dorized, but they retained an unmistakably musty
aroma which attracted all their wild and fully endowed
cousins in the neighborhood. Many a dog suffered a
double dousing in those days, first from a visiting skunk,
then from strong soap and water in the laundry tub.

In spite of their tendency to insult our noses, Jasper
and Minerva made charming companions. Cee's great
amusement was to saunter through the door during a
party on the porch, with her matched pair waddling at
her heels. Her entrance proved particularly effective
among Paul's political friends, most of whom had had
little or no warning about Cee. One guest was so sure
he had a case of the DT's he fled at once and never
came back. Indeed the skunks were a striking two-
some with their snappy black eyes, their wedge faces
crowned with white, their frank white stripes running

from head to tail. When content they buzzed softly in their throats; when aroused the buzz became a sharp trill, not unlike an angry squirrel. Their first reaction to an enemy, be it dog or human, was to turn tail—but not to run. Once those white-tipped brushes were raised there was a significant pause. If the enemy ignored the grace period and pursued his attack, the skunks ducked their heads between their front paws, lifted their hind legs off the ground, and prepared to spray—only with Jasper and Minerva this was always an empty gesture.

They were also intelligent; in fact, it was a heady combination of sense and scent that finally ended their residence at Willowcroft. Since they were allowed to run with the dogs in the backyard, it was not long before they learned the function of the dog door leading from the yard to my parents' bedroom. On one of her rare and reluctant inspections of the back quarters, Nana discovered Jasper and Minerva curled up on Paul's pillow fast asleep. Even for a confirmed antivivisectionist this was too much; Nana stomped out with threats to disinherit her daughter if she brought one more animal into the house. Cee thought it over and this time, for the sake of diplomacy, decided to give away her skunks.

A few years after the departure of Jasper and Minerva, a small crate arrived at Willowcroft. If you looked closely, you could see a long nose poking between the slats, two glittering black eyes, and a domed head with small, flat, round ears. The creature was covered with brown wiry hair, and its humped back tapered into a long tail ringed like that of a raccoon, about the thickness of a broomstick. Its name was Sherman, a coatimundi whose home was in the south, somewhere in Latin America.

When fully grown Sherman weighed about six pounds, the size of an average cat. His feet, which resembled a bear's, bristled with curved, unretractable claws. His underside, of a reddish brown that started at the tip of his lengthy chin and spread like a bib across his chest and belly, was more striking than his topside, yet the coatimundi could hardly be called a beauty. Furthermore, he did not believe in putting on a false face for anyone. One of his frequent gestures was to lift his nose and rubbery upper lip and rapidly click together an inch of yellow teeth, a grimace of pure pleasure, for Sherman indulged in this expression every time someone scratched his back. His back always itched. And, definitely, he smelled.

Physically unattractive as he was, Sherman was a perfectly respectable pet, for anyone willing to take on a coatimundi for a pet. Cee was willing to take on anything. However, until she completed some complicated transactions with Bruce, she was only allowed to consider herself Sherman's foster mother. Until the day he arrived at Willowcroft, the coati's childhood had been far from settled.

No one is sure how Sherman made his way from his native country to a Colorado pet store. There he was purchased by a young Denver couple as a mutual wedding gift. But no sooner was he introduced to his new home than he was thrown out by the bride's parents, an act which boded little good either for the coati or the marriage. A friend told Bruce about the unhappy turn of events, and overcome by a rush of humanitarianism, they scraped together the $50 needed to buy Sherman and carried him triumphantly home to the plush penthouse apartment they were sharing with four other young men. This was my brother's first and last experiment in communal living. His friends took one whiff of the new roommate and threatened to leave without paying their share of the fast-accumulating rent. The ultimatum was never realized, for the landlord evisted the whole group without further ceremony. In the meantime, Sherman was deposited at Willowcroft for safekeeping. Cee was delighted to volunteer her tender loving care.

Bruce lost no time in taking advantage of the situation. As Cee's devotion to Sherman became her Achilles' heel, Bruce became skilled at the art of blackmail. He and his friends had returned to their respective homes, since they had been turned away from every respectable apartment house. For Bruce, Sherman was a sure guarantee of bread and board at Willowcroft. A typical exchange between mother and son would go something like this:

CEE: "Will you clean the corrals tonight?"

BRUCE: "I've got a date."

CEE: "The manure wagon's overflowing."

BRUCE: "Can't—don't have time."

CEE: "You don't seem to have time to do anything around here."

BRUCE: "Maybe I better leave then."

CEE: "That's a fine idea—and take your horses with you. I can use the stalls."

BRUCE (with deliberate articulation): "I'll take Sherman with me too."

Cee (crossly defeated): "Oh, all right. Never mind then."

But if Cee's weak point was the coatimundi, Bruce's was his wallet. In a desperate moment, feeling broke and dispirited, Bruce sold his share of Sherman to Cee for $25, thereby losing all his negotiating leverage. What happened to the share belonging to Bruce's friend remains obscure: at any rate, Sherman took up permanent residence at Willowcroft as one of Cee's chosen.

At first Sherman was removed from his cage only for cleaning and display. Handling him could be an uncomfortable business, for his claws, made for digging in the ground and clinging to branches, were inclined to dig and cling a little too firmly in human flesh. This didn't seem to bother Cee, who was soon wearing long red scratches on her arms and Sherman around her neck like last year's fur. Bruce and Sherman never became so cozy. But the coati loved to drape himself over Eolis's shoulder and nuzzle her in the ear. Sometimes at night when he was tired he cuddled in Cee's lap, his eyes closed, his nose plunged deep into the bend of her elbow.

When it became apparent that Sherman considered his cage home base, he was let loose each day to play in the trees under the watchful eyes of Cee, Nana, Eolis, or whoever was around to baby-sit. Many a hot, windless afternoon the apple trees beside the front porch shook with inner turmoil, to the bewilderment of visitors who were even more astounded when a long ringed tail looped from the branches like a jungle creeper and a dark snout poked from among the leaves.

One of Sherman's favorite sports was to drop on

whatever happened to pass innocently beneath his tree. Often it was a dog, which would whirl in hysterical circles in a futile attempt to dislodge its unwanted passenger, then fly yelping for the house. Often it was Paul, who was equally active and verbal. With Bounty, the boxer, however, Sherman arrived at an amiable understanding. Like Sherman, Bounty suffered from an everlasting itch. She soon discovered that a coatimundi on her back was not altogether an unpleasant sensation; in fact, his tough, curved nails combing her hide were just the answer to her dry skin problem. Every day Sherman went for a jog on Bounty until he became so expert an equestrian he was able to ride his charger, if not into the sunset, at least through the dog door onto the back porch. It was not long before he taught himself how to poke it open with his nose.

If Sherman were in an accommodating mood, he might play in the trees an hour or two, then crawl down a trunk into Cee's or Eolis's arms. More often he would scramble to the top of the tallest cottonwood just as Cee was ready to hurry off to a lunch date or a horse sale. Hours of calling, coaxing, and cursing were spent getting Sherman out of trees. Although he gave no indication of straying, there was always the chance he would drop in the road and get hit by a car. One time in a fright he ran across the road, through a neighbor's yard, and up the neighbor's leg. With admirable composure and few words, the neighbor returned Sherman at once.

He also learned that the shortest distance from the ground to Cee's shoulder, if she was sitting with Nana upstairs, was up the apple tree and onto the railing surrounding the porch roof on the second floor. Often

Sherman amused himself by teetering along the railing as fast as he could while Nana stood behind the safety of her screen door clucking in concern. Other times he would join Nana, Cee, and the cluster of little dogs all sitting on the porch roof in the sun. He never tried to jump on Nana—perhaps she was too frail and powdered for a coati's robust taste.

Sherman took constant watching. An empty cage and quiet trees meant trouble. Several cars were always parked in the circle by the back door; one day not one of them would start. Unable to believe that all the batteries had expired at the same time, Bruce and Paul probed beneath the hoods while Cee beat the bushes in search of Sherman. It was not long before the problem was solved: every coil had been disengaged from the distributor caps in the cars inspected. Sherman was found nestled deep in the engine of Paul's Ford, clutching a coil he had just plucked.

From then on members of the family automatically checked under the hood before going for a drive. But visitors were constantly puzzled when their engines went dead. One day a friend left her car parked in the circle while she and Cee went out to lunch. When she returned, she found that her keys had mysteriously disappeared from the ignition. Sherman was immediately suspect, and sure enough, his cage was empty. Since the friend was in a hurry to get home, the search did not center on Sherman but rather on her keys, which were soon located in the engine. When she fished them out she saw that her oil stick was missing. She drove off anyway, and just as she did she saw the coati poke a narrow, inquisitive face from under the fender of Paul's Ford, where he'd been taking a nap on a front tire.

After that people were instructed to park at the barn and raise their hoods before they departed.

During his first two summers at Willowcroft, Sherman spent much of his time leaping about in the trees. But the third summer he fell from a branch and injured his spine, which confined him more and more to his cage. At night and during the winter he resided in the laundry room, which, with the addition of Amy the raccoon and Samantha the kinkajou, began to resemble the small mammal house at the zoo. Until Samantha ripped it apart, Sherman convalesced curled in a tin dishpan suspended from the top of his cage. He felt very much at home in his pan, sleeping for the most part, occasionally lifting his nose to rapidly click his teeth. If anyone came to see him he would jump out and press his back against the side of the cage to be scratched. Sherman's happiness was then complete, and he would nibble his front paw in pure ecstasy until his benefactor had had enough.

He was still let out for exercise and, in spite of his bad back, proved himself to be as destructive as ever. My first introduction to Sherman took place in the kitchen. Within thirty seconds he had leaped across the floor, climbed my leg, thrust his snout in my shirt pocket, tossed out all my cigarettes, jumped from my shoulder to the telephone nook, knocked the phone to the floor, climbed the hot water pipe to the ceiling, slid down the pipe, and leaped from the floor to the kitchen table sending magazines, pencils, market lists, check stubs, and salt and pepper flying in all directions.

"What *is* it?" was all I could gasp.

He was equally devastating when confined to the laundry room. No matter how cleverly Eolis hid the five-pound box of detergent, Sherman managed to find it and make himself a blizzard which took hours to clean up. After each of these escapades he had to be bathed. For some reason he didn't seem to be colorfast; his undercoat in particular was prone to run, and by the time he was lifted out of the tub and wrapped in a towel, the water had turned a bright orange. For diversion he enjoyed filching the strainer from the dryer, which he then deposited along with rags, empty soap boxes, Paul's sock stretchers, and other objects in a barrel in the corner of the room. Then, curling his tail about him, he settled down among his furniture for a nap. Anyone who tried to extricate him was greeted by ominously clicking teeth. Even Cee's charisma failed when Sherman wanted his way. But Eolis could persuade him to do anything. Slipping on gloves and an old sweater, she would croon sweet nothings to the obstinate coati before she fearlessly plunged her arms into the depths of the barrel. In no time Sherman would be slung across her shoulder, blinking at his sudden emergence into light.

If it had not been for his nose and jaw, which resembled an anteater's, Sherman might have been a quiet animal. He moved soundlessly except when he was knocking things over. His voice, when he spoke at all, was a mere squeak. But his eating habits were notoriously noisy; you could hear him smacking on a peanut butter sandwich and guzzling his orange juice three rooms away. He also possessed an insatiable sweet tooth, and a piece of cake or an eclair was bound to increase the volume of Sherman's normal mastication. Furthermore, he delighted in accompanying his oral cacophony by banging his water dish, an empty tuna fish can, against the side of his cage. In his native haunts Sherman might have made a meal of grubs and berries; here, his staples were raw eggs, grapes, raisins, and peanut butter. How corrupted he was by domesticity no one can tell, but he seemed to thrive at Willowcroft. At any rate, the coati's vitality was inescapably apparent.

Bruce was responsible not only for introducing Sherman to Cee; he must also be credited with rescuing Amy, the next member to join Willowcroft's "wild animal" club. One evening when the family was sitting on the front porch, there was a screeching of brakes outside the side gate. Bruce rushed out and found two boys scrambling about in the road trying to catch something. In a few minutes they came up with a tiny raccoon they had nearly hit. Bruce carried her to the porch by the nape of the neck and put her in one of his old rat cages. Then he put on a leather glove and started petting her. Instead of cowering in a corner she came right into his hand. Apparently she had no fear of either people or the dogs.

Every four hours Cee fed the raccoon two ounces of milk, and she would purr like a kitten and dig her claws in and out. In the morning she felt at home enough to play with a tennis ball. She was about the size of a two-month-old kitten; Cee estimated she must have been about six weeks old. Paul named her Amy, though there was some controversy as to whether or not she might be an Amos.

Amy was to remain Amy, however. If she had any anxiety about her adoptive family, it did not hinder her appetite. She spent most of her first week at Willowcroft eating and twittering; occasionally, when startled, she ducked her head and covered her eyes with her tiny paws. At feeding time she would lie on her back, open her mouth, and cup her tongue to receive the warm jets of milk squeezed from a baby-doll bottle. The milk apparently passed directly into her stomach, for she never seemed to swallow or suck. As her digestion developed she indulged in raw eggs, dog biscuits, grapes, cherries, and as many sticky buns as she was allowed. Amy was a dentist's nightmare; she would have preferred to live on honey alone. Unfortunately, the sweeter grew her tooth, the crosser grew her disposition.

From the beginning Amy showed signs of a flaring temper. Whatever her enemy, a passing dog or a cricket in a crack, she would blow herself up until she looked like a spiny woodland nut, flatten her ears, and advance upon the opposition sideways in short, jerky hops. Even in full bristle she was hardly bigger than a man's hand. When she played she was just as spirited. She amused herself for hours batting Ping-Pong balls around the porch. One of her great pleasures was to ride on Cee's shoulder, in Sherman's seat, clutching the strands of my mother's none too carefully brushed hair.

Like most raccoons Amy had a well-developed sense of touch and was unusually skillful with her paws. A stone dropped in a water bucket was an excuse for an impromptu fishing spree; she would plunge her forelegs in the water and swish them back and forth until she retrieved the stone. After that she would rub it industriously between her front paws as she gazed dreamily into space, thoroughly absorbed in the cold, hard object in her grasp. Contrary to belief, this ritualistic scrubbing was not so much a matter of cleanliness as pure sensation. A peanut or marble pushed under the rug would engage Amy for hours; she would pull it out, look at it, feel it, pat it, then push it under again, only to repeat the whole performance. Once Cee was amazed to see the young raccoon rear on her hind legs and clap her paws together in an unsuccessful effort to catch a fly buzzing about her ears.

Amy slept in the rat cage on Bruce's porch until she learned to unlock her gate and wedge through the screen door into my parents' quarters. After she had demolished their living room a few times, she was removed to a large cage outdoors which she shared with Sherman. On chilly evenings the two cousins cuddled warmly together in a barrel suspended from the top of the cage. When winter came Sherman was shifted to the laundry room and Amy to the barn, where another barrel was hung from the ceiling for her, but she preferred to sleep in a manger. For diversion she leaped about the rafters and ran back and forth across the tops of the stalls. One snowy day she scuttled up the roof of the red barn, slipped, and tumbled down in an avalanche of snow, to the amusement of Cee and the great panic of the horses huddled in the corral.

During her first winter Amy enjoyed her unrestricted nights in the barn so much that she was constantly at the point of abusing her freedom. Cee described a typical incident in a letter to me:

> The other night I called Verna. While we were talking [someone on] the party line started tossing the phone around, blowing in it, and making so much noise we could hardly hear each other. Verna told them she was going to

report them as she'd had constant trouble with them. After we'd talked much longer than we'd wanted to, getting madder and madder, she decided I was to hang up my receiver and she'd leave hers down and just let them wait for the line since they were so rude. When I tried to make another call my line was still connected and I couldn't get through. I tried off and on for an hour, then I finally gave up and went to bed. I lay there puzzling why the connection wasn't broken, when I suddenly realized that the whole answer to the thing was Amy, who spends the evening loose in the barn. She was the one blowing through the phone [at the barn] and dropping it—patting it and knocking it against the wall. Sure enough, the next morning the phone was on the floor. I quickly called Verna not to report the party line.

Amy eventually lost her nightly barn privileges and was permanently confined to the laundry room. Cee let her out for a romp whenever possible. Although she was of average size for a mature raccoon, with a glossy gray-brown coat and a striking black mask, she was heavy and strong enough to be a formidable antagonist when angered. Even Cee had to use her conciliatory arts with Amy to avoid an occasional snap on the finger. Never as domestic as a cat or a dog, she was, in her way, dependent for a wild creature, foraging here and there when released from her cage but never ranging far from Cee or the barn. Only once did Amy venture from Willowcroft to try her fortune in the wild world. No one knows how far her travels took her, or what she thought of providing her own food and water, but after a week during which the family gave her up for dead, Amy sauntered through the dog door into the bathroom while Paul was shaving and greeted Cee with a lick on the nose. Though her coat had lost its luster and she was thinner, she appeared to be healthy and quite content to resume her half-wild life among the dogs, cats, and human beings. But then no one had ever been certain just who was captive at Willowcroft and who was not.

When Amy was a year old, cousin Samantha joined the group, adding an interesting variation on raccoon behavior. Remotely related to both Sherman and Amy, Samantha was a kinkajou by species, a warm-blooded native of South America. Her migration north had been as haphazard as Sherman's, and she had already been through several owners when Cee got wind of her. Since Samantha was extremely sensitive to cold weather, she could not go outside for exercise; therefore my room, kept neatly in order for occasional visitors, was designated for her winter playground. I first learned of the new arrangement in a letter.

"How do you like sharing your room with a kinkajou?" wrote Cee in her usual ex post facto way. Whatever I was supposed to be sharing it with sounded like something to do with the common cold, but I continued to read, warily.

> She's awfully cute. The only problem is she wakes up about the time I go to bed. Then she wants to play. She leaps all around and then gets my hand in her mouth and does all kinds of gyrations. She's about Sherman's size, and is a third member of the raccoon family. She has a lot of gestures like Amy—such as feeling with

> her foot and looking in the opposite direction.
> She is sweeter tempered than Amy and so far
> I've never heard her make a noise. She's a year
> and a half old. I bought her from a sergeant's
> wife whose husband is going to Viet Nam and
> who has to move to Texas. . . .

Naturally no reasonable human being would want to
live in Texas with a kinkajou, I agreed. "I was afraid
she [the kinkajou] wouldn't adjust," continued my
mother, "but if being rowdy is a sign of happiness
she's doing fine."

At this point I closed my eyes and tried to visualize
my room as it had once been in the dear days of my
youth. There was the quilted canopy bed festooned
with horse show ribbons, the long shelf holding a few
tarnished trophies, the gauzelike curtains framing floor-
to-ceiling windows, the neat dressing table, the orderly
desk, the immaculate bureau, the well-arranged bookcase. . . . On I plunged:

> They [kinkajous] are *supposed* to be unde-
> structive and quiet, pleasant pets, but Samantha
> turns the house upside down. Her tail is pre-
> hensile, and if it isn't hanging on to something,
> her hands are. In her jumping ability she more
> resembles Sherman. I imagine she's a tree
> dweller where a raccoon isn't. [Amy, of course,
> was a house dweller.]

And my room? That information, since it was pertinent, somehow never got into Cee's letters. When I
arrived in Colorado the following summer, I found Samantha relocated in the laundry room and my room
completely redone, from new wallpaper to new cur-

tains. Slowly the facts emerged: Samantha had taken full advantage of her playground upstairs by chewing the fringe off the canopy bed, sliding down the four posts, hanging by her tail next to my old coat in the closet, and digging herself a nest in the underside of my mattress. That hole remains as witness to her industry. Undestructive—hardly. She had not spent her first night at Willowcroft before she escaped from her cage, tipped over all the lamps in the front living room, and shattered Nana's best vase.

Yet Samantha cannot be blamed entirely for the nocturnal mayhem that took place upstairs that first winter. As I learned from another letter, Sherman and Amy were lively accomplices:

> I'm up in Samantha's room [no longer my room] where I entertain her every evening. I have brought either Sherman or Amy along to amuse her. She'll play as long as anyone will play with her. Amy gets her under her, then like a woolly umbrella hovers over her and completely obliterates her but for her tail. They galump around the room, Samantha leaping high into the air and landing like a ton of bricks, while Amy just galumps. Sherman likes to get on my lap and of course she comes too and they roughhouse. Samantha will take his nose gently between her hands and nibble on it. When she gets a little rough, he buries it in my turtleneck sweater while I comfort him and croak to him—you can hardly call it singing.

Samantha's keen desire for play was encouraged in part by Cee's equally keen appreciation of her high jinks. Before she came to Willowcroft, the kinkajou had apparently shown little inclination to romp. During an evening upstairs, she'd become so excited she'd scamper in circles about the room, like a red weasel, interrupting her headlong dash just long enough to pounce on Cee's aromatic foot, well seasoned from the barn. Her high spirits, however, were almost her undoing. One evening she took a chill and was discovered collapsed outside her basket panting for air. Her temperature was 102 degrees, 4 degrees above normal. She was rushed to the vet's and put in an oxygen tent. The next day Cee visited her with a bunch of grapes, which she ate. Soon she was able to come home, equipped with a hood designed by the veterinarian which covered her cage, and a 100-watt bulb to keep the temperature at an even 72 degrees. Within a few days Samantha was back at play, none the worse for her bout with pneumonia.

When winter turned to spring and I threatened to appear, Cee began to have misgivings about the condition of the playground. Accustomed to parting with hundreds of dollars for a horse or winter hay, she was appalled at the cost of a new bedspread and curtains. After her financial setback she reluctantly changed the nightly workout to the laundry room downstairs. Though smaller, it offered such challenges as tubs, buckets, mops, detergent boxes, and the wash in progress, not to mention Sherman's well-furnished barrel.

Every evening at ten Cee sallied forth to feed and fondle her wild animals. With loud slurps and much clicking of teeth, Sherman guzzled his orange juice, then climbed through the open door to the top of his cage to watch Amy and Samantha stuff themselves with sweet rolls. One night I followed Cee and found myself in the middle of a happening. At once Sherman tried to jump on my head; when I ducked he ran up his cage and grabbed the light switch. As Sherman switched the light on and off, Samantha slunk in and out among the pipes, up my leg, across my shoulders, and down my side. At the same time Amy made repeated dives for Cee's ankles and then suddenly ended up in Samantha's arms, rolling and twittering across the floor. Cee took in the whole scene with an indulgent smile—after all, it was simply a variation on a constant theme. As for me, I felt I was truly home at last.

9

Friends and Intruders

"SOME OF MY best friends have been made selling horses," Cee often said. One of her major channels of communication was the Sunday *Denver Post* classified section. Every Sunday she advertised what she had for sale and what trades she would consider. About lunchtime people would start pulling into Willowcroft to look around. Since each strange car or truck harbored a potential buyer, Cee was quick to drop her fork and hurry to its side while Paul sighed and resigned himself to a day of interruptions. Concrete business transactions might be few and far between, but the friends Cee made through her ads were many. After the first five minutes, when visitors discovered that her muscular forearms and blunt replies were as harmless as her individuality was refreshing, they not only spent the afternoon but returned week after week, to ride or just to hang around the barn. Age and sex made little difference—the main thing Cee shared with her "manure" crowd was a dedication to animals in general, horses in particular.

Though many had moved away from Denver, Cee's childhood companions had not forgotten her either.

One old friend always timed her trips from New York for the spring so she could sleep in the barn and watch for new foals. During the day she and my mother would brush one horse after another, filling the aisles with dusty heaps of dead hair as they exchanged confidences over the backs of the itchy, shedding animals. Another, who always arrived from Washington dressed in her smartest outfit, was disappointed if Cee didn't pick her up at the airport with a horse in the back of her truck to deliver someplace.

David, Marilyn, and the boys were regular visitors too. They had been living in Germany when their first son was born, and Scott was almost two before they were able to present him at Willowcroft. Nana told me the story of their visit, how Cee had dreaded Scott's arrival for weeks beforehand. Maternal as she was toward colts or calves or puppies, she was always fidgety around human babies, who invariably squealed if she laid a calloused palm on them. Furthermore, the existence of Scott thrust Cee into a category she was reluctant to admit.

"Just so he doesn't call me Grandmother," she growled again and again. "That would be the last straw."

Scott, however, was too young to call anybody anything. When at last the family drove into Willowcroft and he was handed out, giggling at the dogs that were licking his legs, it was Nana who took him in her arms. Cee stood back with a forced smile but with aversion written all over her face. Marilyn had so proudly looked forward to introducing her firstborn to the family that she could not help shedding a few tears of disappointment over the coldness of his reception.

"Don't worry," Nana consoled her. "Sooner or later Cynthia will succumb to his charm. Just be patient."

The next morning Cee rode up to the house where Scott was playing and reached down and put him on the horse in front of her. Since the child had never been near a horse before, he screamed with fear. Cee dropped him off and galloped away without a word but with such a disgusted expression that Nana feared Cee had reached a point of no return.

Several days later Marilyn asked Cee to baby-sit while the rest of the family went to lunch at the country club. Almost as soon as they'd left, Scott had an accident, which was too much for Cee; she was more accomplished at mucking out a stall than changing a diaper.

"I think baby-sitting is for the birds," she informed the family when they returned. "No more for me."

Fortunately, Marilyn was intrepid. With David's support, she once again risked her mother-in-law's ire by humbly asking her to look after Scott while they went to dinner with friends. Cee grumbled but agreed. Since it was chore time she took Scott to the barn with her and parked him in a manger for safety. When she went back to check on him a few minutes later, he was playing contentedly with a wisp of hay, covered from head to toe with large black flies. In the interest of health Cee decided she'd better put him somewhere else, so she closed him in the tack room at the end of the Big Building and opened the top half of the Dutch door. This arrangement worked well for a while until one of the horses ambled into the stable and inquisitively stuck its head over the door and into Scott, causing loud howls. The only thing left for Cee to do was to take Scott with her. Hoisting him to her hip she held him with one hand, then picked up a pail of oats with the other. This was how Nana found her, balancing bucket and baby, when, prompted by misgivings, she made a very rare appearance at the barn. Both faces were so seriously concerned with the tasks at hand that Nana sat down on a bench nearby and laughed until the tears came. However, the barrier had been broken. The next time the family went to the club, Cee offered to stay with Scott.

When they returned a rather startling picture greeted them. Cee was shoveling manure into the cart and Scott was helping her. She was using her shovel and he his hands, which he stuck into the manure, returning with both fists full which he then emptied into the cart. He was jabbering at the top of his voice and Cee was answering him in the same manner.

"Coochie, pookie, hi?" inquired Scott.

"Certainly, we will go tomorrow," replied Cee.

"Doodie, daddie, dar?" he asked.

"Yes, in our car," his loving grandmother assured him.

Marilyn was so happy at their rapport that she never flinched at her son's dirtiness or smell. Cee and Scott remained good friends for the rest of the visit. Nana would watch them fondly from her window as they went about the chores together, Scott riding on Cee's hip or perched on her wheelbarrow—on top of what Nana dared not guess.

As for me, for as many summers as I'd been re-turning to Colorado, I invariably suffered from culture shock, my eastern suburban routine (including a single cat) having ill prepared me for the abundance of animals greeting me at Willowcroft's gate. My mother would respect my delicate frame of mind and treat me more like a guest than flesh and blood for a few days. Then when she thought I could take it, she would proudly usher me to the barn to show off her newest treasures. One year I nearly took the next plane home.

It began innocently enough on a bright June morning after a particularly tiresome flight to Denver the day before. As I walked toward the barn I attempted to adjust my winter-bleary vision to the unfiltered Colorado light. For several years a hollow in the pony corral had been filled with water covered by a skin of algae and insect larvae so thick you could almost walk on it. That day, beneath the brilliant sun and cobalt-blue sky, the pond resembled a lethal lime pie. Suddenly, from around the corner of the red barn, flashed a sidewinder missile, white, puffed, hissing, headed unmistakably in my direction.

"Say hello to Samson," said Cee as if she were making introductions at a party, while I fled up the ramp to the relative safety of the Big Building, my instincts for self-preservation on ready alert. "He'll stop," she reassured me, "if you do. He's Chinese. Isn't he cute? I got him to put in the pond."

"Damn," I gasped. As Cee approached the bird, cooing in her special lingo, Samson lifted his snappy orange beak and evil head from ground level and stretched to his full goose height. He stood no taller than her waist, but there was something as sinister and unpredictable about him as a wolf in sheep's clothing, at least to my wary eye. What we were radiating was anything but goodwill.

Cee finally came up with a halfhearted apology. "He's just a little cross," she explained, nodding toward the little tenant house. "His wife's nesting." Sure enough, tucked in the angle of two walls was a motionless hump of white feathers, what I presumed to be Samson's mate.

"Delilah hasn't moved for weeks—he's antsy, that's all. They ought to hatch pretty soon."

"Great," said I, all enthusiasm.

"He never bites me. Just be nice to him," suggested Cee, as she leaned over and tickled Samson on his long throat.

If I had ever thought about being nice to a Chinese gander, it was too late; we were already engaged in cold war. It was soon apparent that Samson was not only defending his mate but all the territory surrounding the pond and adjacent corral which he had mapped out for the two of them, the very ground I had walked over unmolested for years. The issue at stake was the freedom of the barnyard itself. Confrontation was inevitable.

It took place the next day. As I sauntered casually toward the red barn, I was not unaware of Samson preening himself beside a mud puddle. When he saw me, he didn't even wait long enough to honk; down went his head, out stuck his feathers, and on he came, his flat splayed feet thwacking the dirt like a pair of orange spatulas. I drew in my breath and stood my ground. A yard in front of me Samson slid to a halt, rose on his toes, and hissed.

"Good boy," I chirped, scowling. I took a discreet step backward. Samson took two steps forward.

"That's a good goose," I cooed. "You stupid beast."

Samson snaked his head from side to side but didn't move.

"Aha!" I had seen just enough karate to realize the stunning effect of sudden action and loud noise— I leaped, yelled, waved my arms, and landed painfully flat-footed just in front of the bird, who by now resembled a long-necked balloon.

Startled, Samson withered a little and turned as if to run.

"Back to your pond, fowl!" I shouted, confident that I'd won the skirmish. I patted my hair in place, hitched up my Levis, and, turning my back on the aggressor, continued my measured march to the barn. I was certain that there could be no compromise with this goose— he must be disposed of with all deliberate force and speed; order must be established at once; law must be maintained. Since I had the courage of conviction and outweighed Samson four to one, I was bound to be the superior power, I reasoned. It was then that I heard the sound that still comes back to me in the middle of dark nights: the slap, slap, slap of goose feet in the dust. With a low hiss, Samson struck me on the exposed flank, a searing, fiery pinch that succeeded in anesthetizing one whole buttock for the day.

"Damn you!" I spun, unhooking the big bird from my rear and sending him skidding on his belly. No sooner had he gotten his legs under him, however, than he charged again, this time full front, his chin (if you could call it that) inches from the ground, wings outspread, bill open. Ready alert failed utterly; I froze on the spot. Clamping my pants with his bill, Samson began to beat me repeatedly on the thighs with the spurs of his wings. Had I been able to retreat, I would have gladly, but at this moment of extreme crisis, not one but both my feet cramped. They might as well have been set in cement blocks. I grabbed the goose by his slender throat and with strength born of desperation twirled him around my head and hurled him into space. As he plummeted earthward in a cloud of feathers Cee swooped under him with outstretched arms.

"Poor Sam! Poor Sam! Did she hurt you?"

Outrage blunted my pain. "He attacked me! He nearly killed me—your daughter!" I really thought I was going to cry. Clutching her goose, which I was sorry to see was still alive, Cee glared at me.

"You could have broken his neck," she said slowly.

"I wish I had, oh, I wish I had," I wailed. "He's not even fit for goose liver paste!" Darkly I limped to the house to count my bruises. In retribution I boycotted the barn for several days.

Habit and curiosity finally overshadowed my hostility to Samson and once again I returned to the field of battle, this time armed with a long stick. Unfortunately, the sight of my weapon scattered the horses to the far end of the pasture. I disturbed the goose as little as possible, but when our paths crossed I made faces, shouted threats, and waved my stick around. Samson respected the club if not me. If I had him in sight, I could bypass him with little more than puffs and hisses, but he seldom lost an opportunity to attack when my back was turned. Slap, *slap,* slap, *slap,* slappity-slap— I was so alerted to the sound of his feet that I could hear him coming a block away. Never again did he catch me off guard. Never could I forgive him his cowardly and sneaky way of fighting.

When Delilah finally hatched her brood of three and climbed off the nest, Samson's humor improved somewhat and he became more preoccupied with his family than with me. Still, I had no desire to venture in for a close look at that little fleet sailing around on their sour green waters. Eventually, Samson, Delilah, and the growing goslings became so possessive of their territory and so cranky toward horse buyers and other strangers that Cee reluctantly shipped them off to a neighbor's irrigation ditch. Had I been present at their eviction, I would have cheered.

There were other Willowcroft regulars besides myself whose lives were not centered around horses, but whose pursuits were often as absorbing as Cee's own. Mr. Blackman, a beeman, was called one summer to remove a troublesome hive of bees from the wall of the Big Building. The bees had developed a particularly keen appetite for Bruce and the dogs. When Cee discovered Mr. Blackman owned a horse they were on common ground. Obviously he enjoyed his work, and he came back again and again to remove bees: from the Big Building, from the fireplace in the main house, from the eaves of the little house, even from the top of a fence post where one swarm landed in an unhappy attempt to establish a colony.

Intent, small in stature, soft-spoken, Mr. Blackman had nerves of steel when it came to handling bees. While we quavered at a safe distance, he'd don his netted hat and gloves and, without hesitation, thrust his hand into a throng of angry insects, searching for the queen. Our bees, apparently, were of a wild Italian variety, darkly banded, emotionally unstable, and easily aroused. His object was not to destroy the hive but to transplant it to a box where he would have access to the honey. He removed the bees in the wall by placing the wide end of a funnel-shaped screen over the crack they used for an entrance so that they could fly out but could not crawl back in. Since bees do not soil the nest, all but the queen were forced to leave sooner or later. The three or four days the bees were alarming the air without shelter or a leader were always bad days for Bruce.

Mr. Blackman seldom waited to catch the wild queen; instead, he sent to Louisiana for a new queen and five attendants, who arrived by mail in a little cage sealed with wax. When enough drones had been funneled out of the wild hive, Mr. Blackman set up his box nearby and established the imported queen and her court inside. His assumption that the bewildered drones would be thankful for a roomy estate and royal privileges proved to be correct, but they were loyal creatures, and it took an entire summer to induce all the wild Italians at Willowcroft to settle down with their Louisiana queens. When they did, the honey flowed.

The swarm on the fence post was an easier proposition: Mr. Blackman simply put his hand into the middle of it, plucked out the queen, and popped her into a box which he placed on a stack of similar boxes next to our neighbor's alfalfa field. His skyscraper hive finally became so laden with bees and honey that it toppled over one day, killing the top queen and putting Bruce in a panic. Though badly stung himself, Mr. Blackman telephoned long distance for a new queen and in a few hours gathered enough drones together to refurbish the hive. The coronation took place only a few hours after the new queen arrived in the mail, and we have sweetened ourselves ever since with her honey and Mr. Blackman's company.

Two blacksmiths regularly shared the tasks of keeping the horses properly shod. One of them, Mr. Mingo, had been coming to Willowcroft for as long as I could remember and in the same car, an ancient black limousine. He was probably one of the few black blacksmiths in the country. Under his baggy pants his legs bowed painfully; against the deep brown of his lined face his eyes were a startling, unmistakable blue. He would work slowly, patiently hammering out shoes on his forge, an old steel drum with a hole in the bottom for coals activated by an electric bellows. When he had the shoe he wanted, he then measured it carefully to the sole of the horse's hoof, which he held tightly between his knees.

Mingo's shoeing might last all morning, for he always reassured his client with handfuls of cattle cubes and many pats on the neck. He talked constantly in a low hypnotic singsong. For this reason he was especially good with skittish colts that had never had their feet trimmed. Sometimes Cee helped Mingo by holding a horse for him; more often she perched on the fence surrounding the little house and listened to his problems. While his trade provided him with the means to support his nine children, it was obviously a labor of love. His great disappointment was when his oldest son ran off with all his shoes instead of taking up his business. He did not conceal his admiration for Cee—never had he seen a woman work so hard, he claimed.

The other blacksmith, Buck, operated with a style dramatically different from Mingo's. His shiny red and white truck could be seen whisking up the drive in the evening, for blacksmithing was an avocation Buck fitted in with his regular daytime job. He could shoe three horses to Mingo's one but without the same precision; he was lean, tanned, wore Levi's and a cowboy hat, and talked in a fast, gossipy syntax all his own.

"That horse's shoes worn down to his socks," he'd comment, chiseling away. Buck tended the feet of every horse at Willowcroft except the show horses, trimming the colts for the first time at three months, a proper job for a cowboy used to broncs. At three years, when they'd been broken to ride and drive, the colts would receive their first shoes.

Shoeing Cee's multiplying herds was a costly business, and Cee's eagerness to reduce expenses had at least as much to do with the Brimmers episode as her loyalty to everyone who had ever bought a horse from her. Early one June morning, ten years after she'd sold them a horse, the Brimmers' rented truck rolled up the driveway. Stallions yelled, dogs barked, and Cee, as she said later, jumped out of bed like a shot out of hell. There stood in the driveway a large yellow U-Haul van towing a decrepit green station wagon filled to the top with boxes and furniture. A jog cart was strapped to the roof of the car. From inside the truck came loud whinnies.

"Hi, Woofey," cheerfully called the driver when he spotted Cee. "Where can we put the horses?"

Since every corral was full, Cee had to make room by hurriedly shifting her livestock. When that was accomplished, Papa Brimmer backed the truck to the loading chute and unbolted the endgate. From an interior no larger than a box stall emerged a young girl and boy: Sharon Brimmer, age twenty-one, weight 200 pounds, and Joey, age seventeen, weight 160 pounds. Behind them followed a pinto three-quarter Arab gelding Cee had sold the family, a small black Shetland pony stud, and, last, a white Arabian stallion.

Amazed, Cee peered into the van where, high on a mattress at the top of the truck, was a magnificent Afghan hound sprawled out in all her aristocratic splendor. Underneath her was stacked the rest of the household furnishings plus numerous plants and cages containing chickens, pheasants, rabbits, banties, ducks, and a small white hamster. From the front of the cab tumbled five Pekingese puppies along with their mother, father, and uncle. And there, relieved of her burden of dogs, sat Mama Brimmer in her none-too-clean gingham frock, all 300 pounds of her, holding a small cage in which sang her little English canary, greeting the sun.

The Brimmers, who had traveled nonstop from Arizona, proceeded to unload their livestock and some folding chairs; then they collapsed in the shade of the lilac hedge. Shortly afterward Papa Brimmer drove off in the green station wagon toward Littleton. Cee offered to stable the two stallions to get them out of the way of her own stallions, who were beside themselves with jealousy and rage at the challenge in their midst. At 12:30 P.M. Mama Brimmer and the children were still sitting by the hedge, surrounded by a little ring of dogs and chickens, and the station wagon had not returned. Cee, who had spent the latter part of the morning talking to the group under the lilacs and playing with the puppies, retreated to the kitchen where I was chatting with Eolis.

"What are we going to do about the Brimmers?" she asked, looking slightly worried.

"What do you mean?" I answered cautiously.

"About lunch. He isn't back yet and they can't take the truck anywhere. I bet they're hungry."

"I bet they are," I said noncommittally.

"What do you think, Eolis? Should we ask them in for a sandwich?" Whenever she was in a dilemma, Cee appealed to Eolis.

"Whatever you want, Mrs. Wolf," answered Eolis none too helpfully. Then she added, "This once."

All three of us were thinking the same thing: if Nana had been there the question of how to handle this gracefully would have been solved. But Nana was away on a trip to New England, and Cee's curiosity was in full flower. She considered taking some sandwiches down to the Brimmers, but then decided that would be rude if we ourselves were eating on the porch.

Just then there was a screech of brakes, and a minute later Paul banged into the kitchen, a dark scowl across his brow. "Damn near killed a chicken." He shook his head, then turned to Cee. "What are you going to do about the Brimmers?" he demanded.

"Invite them to lunch," meekly answered Cee.

"Well, I'll have my lunch in the back room, thank you," Paul announced as he stalked through the door.

I nearly followed him—it was evident, even in the open air, that the Brimmers were all badly in need of baths—but I didn't have the heart to abandon my mother to the consequences of her hospitality. In a few minutes Cee, in Nana's chair, Sharon, Joey, Mama Brimmer, and I were seated stiffly at the table on the front porch while Eolis served us sandwiches and iced tea. As Eolis returned to the kitchen, Mama Brimmer's admiring gaze wandered through the open door into the dining room.

"You sure have some pretty things," she said. "I bet they cost a lot of money."

Nana would have been livid. One just didn't say such things.

Mama Brimmer appeared to be the only one of the company in a talkative mood, and she unfolded a long tale of woe about her family's financial problems and their many moves since they were last in Littleton ten years ago. "But we don't aim to intrude, Mrs. Wolf," she assured Cee. "We don't mean to put you out. We're not that kind. The animals needed a rest and we know how much you liked that little horse you sold us awhile back. You said if you could do anything for us . . . well, we hoped we could leave the horses here just until we find a place to live."

Cee's mouth dropped open. "But every stall is stuffed. I don't even have enough room for my own. . . ."

Mama Brimmer seemed to be slowly deflating in her chair. "Sharon and Joey'd take care of them so you wouldn't have to worry none." The two children looked up sullenly from their plates. "They just finished blacksmith school in Arizona," continued Mama Brimmer, gathering confidence. "They could do some shoeing for you."

Cee was silent a moment. All her horses needed to be shod or their hooves trimmed. I knew she'd given in even before she said reluctantly, "O.K., we'll see. If it's only for a day or two."

Three days later the U-Haul truck was still in the driveway. Papa Brimmer had been fortunate in finding a job as a machinist, but no one was willing to rent a house to his migrating family and company. The little establishment on the lawn not only began to look permanent, it appeared to be flourishing. One by one things kept emerging from the truck seeking the sun. Cages full of fowl and a small greenhouse-worth of plants, including strawberries, tomatoes, and peppers, were soon spread out all over the grass. Nobody could figure out where the two immense children had sat during the trip. While their father was at work and their mother under the lilacs, they wandered about the place, fed and watered their animals, and once in a while shod a horse for Cee. Bruce was shocked the first time he discovered Sharon bending over one of the show horses, a hoof clenched firmly between her knees.

"She's going to ruin everything on the place," he sputtered to Cee. "They'll all be lame. Why are you letting these people camp here, anyway?"

Cee wasn't sure herself. But the sight of Mama Brimmer sweating in her chair with a puppy in her lap, or a little pan with a banty chicken in it balanced on her stomach, defied any thoughts of dislodgment. As more time passed the Brimmers slipped away to eat, sleep, and occasionally bathe, but they were back in the morning. Though Paul's frown got deeper and deeper, he refused to discuss the matter with Cee; clearly the Brimmers were her problem. Apologetically she rose to their defense—after all, it wasn't their fault they couldn't find a place to live, the kids were a help, and Papa Brimmer had promised to fix the corrals and paint the fences, which was more than anyone else was willing to do. The truth was the children did as little work as possible, letting Cee take care of their animals as well as her own. Papa Brimmer's promises were just that. But Cee stubbornly refused to recognize what was happening. If she didn't have the courage to tell the family to leave, neither did the rest of us; we tacitly assumed it was up to her. When it became crucial that the Brimmers unload the rest of their belongings and return the U-Haul truck, Cee tried one more tactic.

For a number of years the small tenant house across from the barn had been nothing but a repository for un-used furniture, much of it belonging to Paul. Cee had been urging him to get rid of the goods. Without Paul's knowledge, she told the Brimmers they could use the little house if they cleaned it up. They were delighted, and the minute Paul left for work they began to shuffle chairs, tables, and desks into another building. Their efforts lasted just long enough to scrape out a place to sleep in case of rain. Paul was furious when he dis-covered his things had been moved and the Brimmers ensconced in the little house, but still he did nothing about them. They spent most of their time outside the house, putting a new fence around it and painting it with white trim. In the corner where the goose Delilah had nested, Mama Brimmer planted a cornucopia of pe-tunias and strawberries.

I recall the scene at the little house shortly before my visit ended that year. In the center of the lawn was a large wire cage in which a buff-colored rabbit hunkered, nibbling grass. Around the base of a nearby willow tree stood a ring of freshly planted pansies and around that a circle of chairs. One chair was com-pletely filled by Mama Brimmer, who had just emerged from the bath clad in a snow-white satin robe (made to order by her daughter), amply fringed with goose down that dipped from her neck to her lap, where it disappeared beneath a Pekingese pup. Occasionally she would pluck at the robe in a modest but futile attempt to draw it across her bosom. My mother, in her customary shorts and striped T-shirt, occupied the second chair with another pup, the late afternoon light silver in her hair. Dogs lay clumped at her feet. Leaning over the new fence he'd almost finished painting was Papa Brimmer in blue overalls.

"Woofey, it was a lucky day we bought that colt from you," he said after a reflective silence.

Cee gazed at the setting sun. "I guess so," she answered weakly.

But one day, like a family out of *The Grapes of Wrath,* the Brimmers disappeared as suddenly as they had come, and it was none too soon. Apart from the fact that they outweighed the Wolfs three to one, Willowcroft, which had proved elastic enough for Cee's livestock, seemed to snap with the strain of an additional truckload of animals and people. The longer the Brimmers lingered, the more morose became the Wolfs. Paul glumly avoided them, and Cee, whose customary affection for her horse buyers had long since worn thin, sulked mutely. Neither she nor anyone else could summon the courage to tell the Brimmers to leave. What could they be blamed for, beyond violating the laws of hospitality?

Then one morning Cee found cause, and it was of a nature guaranteed to produce results. A mare that Sharon had shod was hobbling painfully around the corral. Close inspection revealed a nail driven into the tenderest part of her hoof. Flushed with anger, Cee straightened up from her examination just as Sharon came into the corral.

"Get out of here," Cee said by way of greeting.

Sharon stopped. "What's the matter?"

"You know damned well what's the matter," hissed Cee. "This is the horse you shod, isn't it? Look at her, she can't even walk. The best show horse on the place, dead lame." Cee's voice rose higher and higher the madder she got. "If I ever catch you . . . if I—"

Sharon's face puffed up and her lip trembled. "Wolf, Wolf, aren't you satisfied with my work?"

"You're damned right I'm not! Couldn't you see what you were doing? Are you so dumb—"

"Don't call me dumb," wailed Sharon.

"I'll call you what I like!" screeched Cee, whose voice was about to break. "Get out of here! All of you!"

She rushed for the barn and Sharon retreated to the little house, both their faces streaked with angry tears.

A few minutes later Mama Brimmer came huffing into the barn to declare they'd have to leave the place as apparently they weren't wanted. She stood before my mother, a mountain of injured dignity, but Cee didn't dare say a word. Instead she became very busy filling water buckets, fiercely formulating her case against the Brimmers. But she never had a chance to recite her catalog of grievances; by the time she trusted herself to speak, the Brimmers had pulled out, returning the next day only to collect their possessions without a word. All that remained of their six-week invasion was a Pekingese pup they'd given Cee earlier. For a year she heard nothing more about them; then she learned they were living thirty miles south of Littleton under a different name. There was something inherently rootless about the family, a suggestion of disorder, failure, and dismal secrets. As for the horse that started it all, that was one sale Cee lived to regret.

10

Pennywise

THOUGH SHE DIDN'T always care to admit it, Cee relied on the people she met for reasons of business as well as of friendship. Very early she realized that a local dealer was as important to her trade as an agent to an actor, and several of her "horse friends," as Nana and Paul labeled them, dated back to her pony-raising days. Cal Jeter, who first introduced Zirra to Cee, was one of these, and his dusty pickup, empty or loaded, was a familiar sight at the barn. He and my mother had an arrangement whereby he would pick up a horse cheap at a sale and she would fatten it up, ride the kinks out of it, and then sell it as a child's horse. They would split the difference of any profit they made. The horse was allowed only one month to complete its shape-up program at Willowcroft; otherwise it began to consume its potential value in hay. Cee and Cal's greatest coup was when he discovered an Appaloosa pony in a farmer's load of cows which he bought for $125. Four weeks later Cee sold it to a family in Texas for $1,300.

As vital to Cee's particular trade as the Sunday ads was the telephone. "What I'm going to get your mother for her birthday is a necklace with a telephone hanging on it," Paul announced to me once. I remember an essay I wrote in grade school beginning, "My mother deals horses over the phone," which was singled out for its misuse of language. If the opening sentence wasn't literally true, it was descriptive enough of her activities for me to justify it, then and always. Long after, on one of my annual visits, I overheard a conversation that went like this:

Telephone rings.
"Hello. . . .
"What've you got to sell? . . .
"Ten what? . . .
"Ten broncs. I can't help you. I've got guests."
Meaning me.
"What about her papers? . . .
"Yeah, but what would I do with her? She's bronchy, isn't she? . . .
"Yeah, but that's a different thing than handling her. . . .
"O.K., I'll give you a ring."

The particular horse dealt over that telephone happened to be an eight-year-old Welsh pony barely halter-broken. If it hadn't been for the look on the houseguest's face, Cee might well have ended up with another blooming child's horse.

The constant struggle to maintain too many animals on too little land frequently forced Cee to defray expenses through some ingenious schemes other than horse trading. Permitting Sharon Brimmer to shoe her horses was one that backfired. Another was a system whereby she leased a mare to someone else for a

two-year period. The lessee had the privilege of riding, feeding, vetting, and paying the insurance premi-
ums on the mare in return for her first year's foal. Cee
kept the second year's foal in the hope that she could
sell it at six months before it began to eat too much.
Unfortunately, a Willowcroft weanling had a talent for
becoming a Willowcroft yearling and eating, alas, like
a horse. Though my mother's leasing activities always
accelerated before my summer visit, she never managed to empty the corrals convincingly or freshen up
the grass.

Until the Littleton Large Animal Clinic was built,
Cee's long acquaintanceship with the local veterinarians furnished her with the opportunity to board sick
horses at Willowcroft in return for a deduction from her
vet bill. The last boarder was a painfully lame quarter-
horse stallion who got thinner and thinner in spite of
all the feed Cee gave him. Every time he threw himself
she had to call the clinic and ask a vet to drive over
with ropes to haul him to his feet. When at the end of
a month he was nothing but bones covered with bed-
sores, he was destroyed. The autopsy revealed a long
open crack across his entire stifle (the joint above the
hock), almost impossible to heal.

Cee was still willing to serve the interests of science
as long as she was paid for it. One day a man called to
ask if she would volunteer for an experiment involving
estrogen being conducted at Colorado State College in
Fort Collins. Cee's job was to collect urine from her
pregnant mares, for which she would receive $5 a gal-
lon. She agreed readily enough when she heard the
price for what went to waste anyway, but how to collect
a specimen from an untoilet-trained horse presented a

problem. Finally she rigged up a long rubber bladder made from an old inner tube which she then harnessed to the rump of the hapless mare. After much kicking and bucking only one mare in the bunch was found who would consent to wear the thing, my pony, Alice in Wonderland.

There were problems. Alice's own bladder functioned at peak capacity, which often caused her artificial one to overflow. Cee had to empty the rubber bladder at least three times a day—not a pleasant task. When Alice trotted in the pasture—and she liked to trot in the pasture—she sloshed so loudly you could hear her at the barn. Visitors immediately pointed to her peculiar trappings and demanded, "What's that?" which involved many complicated explanations from Cee. Alice was finally relegated to the farthest field out of sight, but still Cee had to tramp out, catch her, and empty the bladder. Gallon jugs of Alice's output were stored in the already cramped tack room until they were collected by the experimenter, who then conducted tests on the precious liquid in his own backyard. Finally his neighbors complained so much that the experiment came to a premature halt, admittedly to Cee's relief. As for poor Alice, her only recompense was a bare bottom where the inner tube had rubbed off all her hair.

Willowcroft's reputation as a biological testing ground remained unblemished, however, and a few years later another researcher appeared from Fort Collins. This particular young student of veterinary medicine was conducting his study on bloodworms, a common horse parasite. Every month he took fecal samples for his tests in return for the free worming of all Cee's

horses. The fecal experiment was a much better arrangement for Cee than the urine experiment, for the
student went directly to the best sources of supply, the
large corral or the four acres, selected those manure
clods that interested him, and carried them back to the
laboratory for scrutiny under the microscope. As luck
would have it, he shipped off to Australia before he
finished his research, and once again Cee had to pay
for worm control.

Every year Mr. Oiler, a "custom farmer" (one who
farms for others), faithfully delivered his entire crop
of hay to the barn, about 500 to 700 bales a cutting.
His second cutting, made up of alfalfa, timothy, and
orchard grass, was usually the best. Any hay that had
become wet, dusty, or moldy he fed to his calves. As
Mr. Oiler was an authority on cows, he and Cee enjoyed carrying on long conversations about cows, occasionally branching into broader subjects such as one's
philosophy of life or naughty stories.

Twice a week old Pat, well up in his seventies, rattled up the drive in his stake truck with a supply of grain
from the Littleton Mills: 200 pounds oats, 200 pounds
sweet feed, 200 pounds compressed hay pellets, plus
salt blocks and minerals. He was so familiar the dogs
didn't bother to bark, even when he pulled in at 9:00
P.M. and heaved the heavy sacks off the back of the
truck into the barn with a deftness that would put a
seventeen-year-old to shame. In spite of his irregular
hours, Pat never missed a delivery.

Cee always winced a little when she got her feed
bill at the end of the month. One summer she decided
she'd supplement her hay and grain with grass clippings

gleaned from neighboring suburbia. This was one of her less successful ventures; not only did cars roll in at all hours with baskets of leftover lawn, but the grass, which was often moist and hot, was gobbled hoggishly by the horses, resulting in catastrophic stomachaches and a vet bill higher than ever.

The worst case of colic I encountered was a direct result of these clippings. It happened during one of the rare times Cee went out of town for a horse show and I volunteered to do chores. I was busily trying to remember what horse went where for grain when I noticed one of the registered Arabs who had been eating grass cuttings all day begin to paw, roll, and look at her sides, all unmistakable signs of colic. I managed to get the mare into a stall just as a farmer with two boys drove up with another load of grass. I yelled at them to hold everything and flew to the phone. Even as I dialed the clinic I heard the mare crash against the wall of the stall; she had cast herself on her back, her four legs rigid in the air. With the help of the farmer and his boys, we managed to roll her over, all 1,100 pounds of her, and to prod her, groaning, to her feet.

The farmer agreed to walk her while I completed as many chores as possible and waited for Dr. Johnson, the large-animal vet. By the time Dr. Johnson arrived, she had buckled at the knees and her neck was dark with sweat. He gave her a shot for pain and she rallied for half an hour. Then she hunched her back and nearly collapsed. By this time I had enlisted a friend to help with the walking since the poor farmer who had come only to drop off his grass had chores of his own to do. As the mare's respiration became faster and faster and her pain increased, Dr. Johnson, who had been watching her closely for more than an hour, became silent. The mare was now drenched from head to tail with sweat and her eyes were glazed. It was impossible to keep her from going down, so we took her to the front lawn where the grass softened her fall when she threw herself. After giving her a series of shots without response, Dr. Johnson shook his head.

A decision had to be made; it was no longer a question of whether the mare would live but how she would die. If she were allowed to die naturally, there would be no doubt about collecting the substantial amount of insurance due on her. But dying naturally might take her all night in considerable agony, and Cee was expected back from the show in two hours. On the other hand, if Dr. Johnson put her to sleep, the insurance company was sure to question his precipitous action and perhaps refuse to pay. But watching the mare thrash on the lawn in the soft summer twilight, we decided to take the risk. Paul made an emergency call to the insurance office in Chicago. We knew we had to get the mare off the place before Cee came home.

Once more we prodded the poor mare to her feet and led her trembling to the horse trailer which had been hitched to my friend's car. So accustomed was the mare to being hauled from show to show that she never hesitated but leaped into the trailer and stood expectantly with her chest braced against the manger. As she weakly lowered her head, Dr. Johnson leaned over the side and plunged a long needle deep into her neck. The mare quivered all over, lurched violently to one side, and went down. In a few minutes she had started on her last ride as car and trailer rolled down the driveway. When Cee returned at 10:00 P.M. the autopsy had already been performed by the clinic staff; they had found a completely twisted intestine for which there was no hope. They also found the five-month embryo of a tiny but perfectly formed filly foal.

The minute Cee got home that night I blurted out the bad news. Her face went slack and the circles under her eyes deepened. "Oh, no," she said. My father patted her on the back and she forced a smile and went into the back room. In a minute she returned to ask how it had happened and to find out the details of the autopsy. Both Paul and I felt the need to protect her, and I realized that was what we had been doing all evening in our urgency to have the mare destroyed and her carcass removed. Once more I had the sensation of being older than my mother. Her stubborn toughness and her childlike vulnerability existed side by side like oil on water; their failure to blend bewildered me. Cee vowed she would never leave the place again or feed grass to the livestock. Within a month she had broken both her promises.

11

Life and Death Matters

THERE WAS some truth to my mother's frequent claim that she supported the Littleton veterinarians. Cee and Dr. Howarth, the small-animal vet, became acquainted shortly after we moved to our first farm in 1947, and over the years Cee called him countless times to treat a cat suffering from feline distemper or to save a dog hit by a car. He was the one who successfully pulled Samantha through her bout with pneumonia. A dark-haired man with a gentle voice, Bill Howarth knew Cee (whom he called Cynthia) as well as anyone in Littleton, and he never failed to offer reassuring words and an arm around the shoulder when an animal died. One summer when I was visiting, I saw how patient and dedicated Dr. Howarth could be.

The trouble started earlier with Tanya, the German shepherd. There was no explanation for the atrocity she and another dog committed one dark night when they crept into the box where Bruce's Australian shepherd, Heather, was nursing eight new purebred puppies. Though the mother fought desperately to defend her family, Tanya and her accomplice killed every puppy. Bruce arrived in time to whip Tanya soundly before she wrenched from his grasp and tunneled into the bushes along the driveway where she spent a fearful night. Had Cee been able to catch either dog she would have taken them both to Dr. Howarth's to be destroyed. But they instinctively eluded all human contact until passions had cooled somewhat. Cee, in the meantime, was forced to turn her attention to the bereft mother.

All night Heather prowled around her empty bed, whining and searching for her puppies. As soon as the sun rose, Cee was on the telephone and for almost eight hours placed call after call in a desperate attempt to find unwanted puppies that Heather could adopt. That evening Dr. Howarth called back to say he had four day-old mongrel pups that had just been brought to him to be destroyed. The real problem now was whether or not Heather would accept these creatures which smelled of strange dog and veterinary clinic.

When Paul entered the kitchen at 7:00 P.M. he found Cee dousing Heather's face and nose with his favorite shaving lotion. The four puppies were already soaked with it. Carefully they were placed in their foster mother's box. Heather sneezed, sniffed, licked tentatively at a puppy, then cleaned it off. By the time she'd finished mopping up the last one, they were all covered with her smell. Heather sighed and lay down to nurse her new brood, diminished from the day before but nevertheless alive.

Heather's adopted family resembled nothing yet at Willowcroft. As they grew, poodle parentage made its appearance in their kinky coats and square, hairy snouts, but their other genes were a matter of debate. They were low and stocky—the two darkest ones bore a marked similarity to Aberdeen Angus. Heather's sister Dawn, who had been party to the murder of the original litter, did penance by baby-sitting like a good maiden aunt. Just after dusk each evening the whole family went for an outing down the driveway to the mailbox and back: first Heather and Dawn, then Cee, then the four tumbling puppies followed by a couple of cats from the barn. On the other side of the fence in the front pasture a red cow and a small black pony strolled along with the group. From a visitor's point of view, the tableau looked as idyllic as the Peaceable Kingdom.

But death once more courted Heather's children and singled out its victim just as suddenly as the time before. One warm quiet night, about an hour after the usual expedition to the mailbox where the puppies romped in high spirits, Cee found one of them lying limply in the backyard. As she picked it up it whimpered and tried to bite; then its eyes rolled back in its head. Though it was now 9:00 P.M., Cee called Dr. Howarth, who was in bed with a bad back. He told her to meet him at his office. On the way over I held the unconscious puppy on my knees and rubbed its stomach while it cried softly. It was gulping for air when we arrived, and Dr. Howarth slipped it immediately into an oxygen tent.

As we waited, Cee and Dr. Howarth rattled on about local people and events. I was surprised at their apparent indifference to the small form gasping for breath under the glass dome, but they were used to the struggle that was going on—and I was not. Occasionally the veterinarian would bend over to adjust the valves on the oxygen tank, then straighten slowly, pain flickering across his face. Cee sat on the counter near the puppy, her arms crossed. Neither one of them could figure out what had happened to it: Dr. Howarth guessed that it might have gone into shock after choking on something, but there was no evidence. Toward midnight its rapid breathing changed into abrupt heaves, spaced farther and farther apart. Cee and the vet were quiet now, from long experience anticipating the end. As I listened to the puppy's last low cries, I knew how far all of us were from that small extinguished world.

"Well, at least it didn't regain consciousness," rationalized Cee as we drove home in the dark.

While Dr. Howarth's specialty was small animals, other veterinarians in the area, such as Dr. Johnson, treated animals larger than dogs, cats, and kinkajous. Hardly a week went by that Cee didn't call one of the four vets practicing at the Littleton Large Animal Clinic. They were so familiar with Cee's horses that they knew them by name. Each vet had a special mobile unit driven by an aide, usually a young intern, which was a modified pickup with an eight-foot covered bed containing emergency medical equipment, hot and cold running water, and a telephone. The unit, belonging to the veterinary association, took an hour to pack. Each truck was a different shade of blue, ranging from bright to dark, so that only a glance was needed to tell which vet was calling. When a truck from the clinic pulled into the drive, everything else was dropped.

Despite the frequency of their visits and Cee's indebtedness to the veterinarians, she administered much of the routine medication herself. With Bruce's help she immunized all her horses, including new foals, against sleeping sickness every spring. Every four months she spooned a dose of worming medicine into each horse's grain. An expert at swabbing out a puncture wound or keeping a colicky horse on its feet until the vet arrived, she more than once saved an animal from permanent injury or even death. If a colt developed distemper, she waited patiently until the egglike lump which formed under its jaw was soft enough; then she lanced it with a sharp knife, releasing a sticky pudding of pus and blood. She felt no squeamishness at performing this operation as long as it saved a vet bill. If an animal appeared to be slobbering its grain more than usual, she knew just how to pry its mouth open and check its teeth to see if they had developed points. Unattended, horses with bad teeth have been known to starve to death. When a mare was in foal, Cee watched her carefully for sickness or injury that might cause abortion.

Cee began each spring with high hopes that her mares would reward her with fillies, easier to sell than stud colts. During the foaling season the vet was on call at any hour, day or night. As mares usually foaled at night or in the early morning, Cee might start sleeping in the barn from March onward. She was a skilled midwife and could even deliver foals with a twisted leg or a shoulder block without calling the clinic. But she knew from long experience that protracted or difficult labor in a mare could spell disaster.

In spite of a few dramatic cases, Cee had reasonably good luck with her broodmares, considering the number of foals that had been born at Willowcroft. Occasionally a foal arrived during the daytime, to the delight of those who were available to witness the event. Spunky the donkey always chose to deliver in the afternoon. She was my first experience with childbirth, and I found no similarity to what I had read or imagined. What astounded me most about the whole process was not that such a large object emerged from such a small opening, but that it was so incredibly fluid. Everything seemed to be wet, bloody, and slippery. So saturated were the little donkey's ears that they hung by the side of its face as limply as a hound's; when they finally popped erect, they were almost twelve inches long, giving it the appearance of a startled jackrabbit.

Once when Spunky was showing signs of imminent delivery Nana was hostessing a bridge party. Cee rushed up to the house to tell her the news. Abandoning their cards, Nana and her three friends supplied themselves with folding chairs, carried them sedately to the pasture fence, and sat down to view Spunky's trial as leisurely as they had seated themselves at the bridge table not an hour before.

Cee could usually tell when a mare was going to foal by her restless behavior. Pacing the fence, pawing, kicking her belly, were all signs of discomfort. Her bag became swollen and hard, and a waxlike substance dripped from the teats. These symptoms might be evident for only an hour before foaling or they might last for days, during which Cee resigned herself to spending her nights in the barn on a cot in front of the expectant mother's stall. "I can hear a mare's water break even in my sleep," claimed Cee. But after years of foaling seasons, sleep had a way of ambushing even the most alert.

Sometimes Cee was able to persuade her friends to share her midwife vigils. On a certain cold March evening, Cee invited two of her friends over to eat leftovers. One of the Arab mares was due to foal, and Cee was so busy running back and forth between the barn and the house, she burned the lima beans three times. When she tried to return to the house, the mare would whinny and mill restlessly around her stall. The only thing to do was to stay with her, but Cee felt guilty about abandoning her guests. Finally she announced, "I've got a swell idea. Let's put my cot in front of the stall and we can sit on it and spread a horse blanket over our knees. We can put the heat lamp by our feet."

This arrangement seemed to satisfy the mare, who dozed off to the sound of chatter and many giggles. As the evening wore on, the three on the cot got colder and colder, and they pulled the heap lamp nearer and nearer. The rosy glow that was beginning to creep over Cee's body suddenly became intense.

"Hey, do you smell something burning?" asked one friend, sniffing. Jumping to her feet, Cee discovered that her long underwear was on fire. She managed to slap out the flames just in time to say good-bye to her companions, who by 2:00 A.M. had grown weary of the whole affair. After peering at the mare through a crack in the adjoining stall, she crawled under the horse blanket and closed her eyes.

The mare yawned, Cee yawned; two stalls away the unsuspecting father crunched hay as if he were grinding two-by-fours, the metal buckle of his halter clanging on his water bucket. The mare's hoof crashed against the side of her stall. Gas, Cee decided. A cat sailed out of the rafters, landing like a cement block on top of the baled hay; the two barn dogs stirred, whined, turned in their beds; the goat rustled and bleated.

Wearily Cee tried to smother the barn noises by covering her head with the blanket, to no avail.

Then all at once everything was very still. Cee saw through the crack that the mare was dozing, her head drooped, one hind foot resting off the ground. Cee lay back with a sigh. She had much to do: a trail ride next week . . . a show after that . . . horses to condition, colts to halter break . . . and another night in the barn tomorrow, no doubt. As she drifted sleepward in a swirl of hay and shavings, the rooster next door plucked his head from under his wing and cocked an eye at the east. Fluttering to the Willowcroft fence, he stretched out his neck and crowed, first tentatively, then triumphantly as the rest of the roosters in the neighborhood joined in. Cee floated over a waterfall and landed with a splash; she jumped off her cot just in time to see the mare scramble to her feet, turn to her newborn foal, and whicker hello. A high, birdlike nicker answered her. Armed with the bottle of iodine she used for painting navels, Cee entered the stall and stared critically down at the wet and panting foal. Gingerly she lifted its tail.

"You goddamned boy!" she cried, giving it a whack on the buttocks. The foal bobbed its nose in the air and regarded her with moist wide-set eyes. "But what a beauty," crooned Cee.

Afflictions such as colic, probably the most common ailment at Willowcroft, flu, worms, and even the uncertainties of foaling Cee was prepared for. "It's all a part of the business," she would say with a shrug. There were also things that went awry which invariably caught Cee off guard, such as the time old Abou aspirated his breakfast and nearly choked to death. Cee hopped him over little jumps she made from fence rails until the vet could come. Abou survived with nothing more serious than a sore throat, requiring a daily gargle of salt water.

Loose wire, nails, and hazards of every description are always turning up to plague a horse owner. One morning Cee found Tishka, her prize-winning half Arab, standing in a pool of blood. She got the mare into a stall, applied a pressure bandage to her torn pastern, and called the vet, who took almost three hours to stitch her up. Tishka had severed an artery and a vein and had lost about 12 percent of her blood. Cee was able to track her across the corral to a shed at one end covered by a sheet of galvanized aluminum siding. The edge of the sheet was coated with blood and hair where Tishka had caught her foot. Had Cee been an hour later, the mare would have bled to death.

Accidents like this one were always a grim surprise for Cee, who tried to eliminate as many dangers as possible. But there were some things that had to be attributed to whatever arbitrary god presides over the equine population, and Cee became more and more fatalistic about the calamities which seemed to ghost every horse. Resigned as she was, she never became superstitious. If her barnyard seemed to be the seat of plague and her vet bill astronomical, she had only to compare herself with other breeders to know she was in good company. But there was one week in August when she was ready to believe that Willowcroft had been singled our for divine retribution. Within seven days, seven of her horses died. It was a loss from which Cee never fully recovered.

Cee entered the corral one morning to find Zirra, her favored Arab mare, carrying her head to one side at a peculiar angle. She came up to Cee and nickered; she appeared not to want Cee to leave her. Cee called Dr. Johnson, who told her to put the mare in a dark stall as her eyes were running and she was blinking them rapidly in the strong sunlight. Everytime a horse snorted or a gate slammed she winced.

Zirra lay down the minute she entered the stall. When Dr. Johnson came, he could see no sign of injury. Cee guessed that a particularly vicious horse she was keeping at the time might have cornered Zirra in the shed and she had reared, striking her head on a beam. Dr. Johnson left, promising to return that evening. Cee checked the mare every hour and was always greeted by a nicker. It was difficult for her to tear herself away, even to eat or sleep.

Two mornings later when Cee started her chores, she was appalled to find the gate between the pony corral and the small lean-to where she kept the grain wide open. Sure enough, a garbage can holding a hundred pounds of oats was overturned and four ponies were staggering around in a state of drunken oblivion while a fifth was already on the ground, its sides hard and distended. Afterward Cee discovered the grain, brought in by a dealer, was poisoned. Though she had been down twice during the night, Cee had noticed nothing unusual because she was so absorbed with Zirra.

Some old friends, a couple we had known in Utah, were visiting at the time. Cee felt that she should be with them, but nothing seemed to matter as long as she could save Zirra. Though Dr. Johnson came twice a day, he could do no more than give the mare a

sedative when she became too restless. Whenever someone touched her she quivered all over as if she had been
stung, and she was constantly moving about the stall.
By the third day she had become noticeably weaker,
no longer able to get to her feet. Cee banked the stall
with bales of straw to keep the mare from banging into
the walls. She hardly noticed when the glutted ponies
expired. She could not admit to herself that Zirra was
dying.

"Just remember, she is only a horse. You mustn't
grieve so if she dies," counseled the visitors. Cee found
their words anything but comforting. Zirra was not only
a horse; she was the horse my mother had sought all her
life. The romantic vein that lay beneath her brusque-
ness had found its outlet in Zirra and in the poetry she
wrote to her. The wound of her death would be deeper
than people could understand.

Six days after Zirra was stricken Dr. Johnson and
Cee were talking beside the corral. Suddenly there was
a squeal and a crack as hoof met bone. They looked
up to see a palomino filly Cee had just bought collapse
in the dust with a fractured skull, kicked by the same
horse that may have cornered Zirra. Cee leaned weakly
against the fence, stunned to the point of indifference.
But her ordeal was not over.

Zirra died at noon the next day. I had arrived
home early that morning, and when Dr. Johnson's truck
pulled in, I went with him to the barn. Cee was sitting
in Zirra's stall as she had been for the last hour, the
mare's head in her lap. Gently she stroked her ears and
murmured to her to calm her, for Zirra was in a state
of hypertension, shuddering and churning with her
front feet.

"Why don't you let me give her a shot, Cee, and put her out of her misery," suggested Dr. Johnson softly.

Cee frowned, "No, not yet. This could be the turning point. Maybe . . ." Her voice trailed off.

Flat on her side with her head in Cee's lap, the mare began to run. Faster and faster her legs moved as if she were racing before a black wind blown from her ancestral home. Then suddenly she was still. Dr. Johnson and I went into the stall and squatted beside her.

"Come on, Mum," I said. "Let's go."

Cee glanced up blankly a moment, then down at Zirra, watching the fog creep into her eyes. She bent over, pressing her face into the tangled red mane, and wept.

It is curious, perhaps, that no animal graveyard was ever created at Willowcroft. The only memorial was a plaque over the door of the Big Building, erected when it was converted into a stable: "Dedicated to the memory of my beloved Zirra." The only grave was a small mound of earth in the backyard under Cee's window where Minnie the Mooch lies buried after dying in Cee's arms not long ago from a heart attack. My mother had never been able to take the death of an animal lightly, but of all of those at Willowcroft, she possessed Zirra and Minnie most completely, and they left a space that could never be completely filled again. Philosophically she knew that time was on her side. But she remarked one day, not without a certain regret, "I wish I wasn't so attuned to animals and more to people—there aren't so many of them one cares about."

12

Flash Flood

WHILE LIFE at Willowcroft was influenced by barnyard accidents, it was also at the mercy of the weather which bounced capriciously off the front range of the Rockies. Winter around the barn could pierce the illusion of anyone who still believed in the pastoral myth of the farm. Whenever a blizzard swept in, an icy path had to be plowed from the house to the barn; pipes froze and had to be thawed by holding a torch of newspaper to them; water consolidated in every bucket; horses bunched and shivered against the swooping wind, their hay buried the minute it was thrown out to them. Snow drifted as high as the eaves of the barn one year, snowing us in for a week, and we had to ride to town for food, a slow trip on horseback but a great boost to the dying pioneer spirit.

The day after a storm the sun would glare blindingly on the blanketed world, while paradoxically the temperature plummeted to subzero. I squeaked out one morning in minus 13 degrees, my toes and fingers numbed on immediate contact with the air. A dog that tried to lick the ice around a water spigot froze its tongue to the pipe. A pony was planted in the corral barely conscious; somehow we managed to stagger her into the barn, where we spent hours vigorously rubbing her with towels to thaw her out. Yet often the snow, before it was trampled and laced with mud, could be quite beautiful. I remember one evening, as thick flakes began to float quietly over the barns and corrals, hearing a chorus of Canada geese. As the honking became louder I realized that a perfect V was flying toward me, barely distinguishable through the whiteness. They were only a few yards above the fences, so low I could see their legs flattened like black slashes against their chalky underbellies, and the air all about me was swept with flight and sound and snow.

Chores in winter were done quickly with much blowing of hands and stamping of feet, but there was more work because more horses were kept in the stalls. Cee went out at six thirty in the morning when it was dark; in the evening she came in at six when it was dark, and the pile of manure beside the barn continued to rise and freeze. Late in February the sun began to send down a little heat—you might see clods steaming here and there. Soon the corrals became sinks of slimy mud and putrid pools, to the enjoyment of the horses, who found a roll in the mud the quickest way to rid themselves of their itchy winter coats. Cee, in knee-high rubber boots, squished along behind her wheelbarrow, which plowed deep ruts in the ground that would freeze solid during the next cold spell. The horses were given their daily airing without blankets, which meant considerable scrubbing and currying afterward. The barn was afloat with old hair and dust. One concession to the machine age was Cee's horse vacuum cleaner, which could inhale the fine, layered dirt at the roots of a horse's hide, once the horse learned to stand the noise and tickle and not to shy at the hose.

Spring weather with its mild days and cold nights stirred the blood. The animals attended to reproduction and the people looked forward to summer shows and rides. But winter usually had one more harsh cough. Periodically in May another snowstorm landed heavily on the leafing trees and shrubs, leaving a wake of strewn boughs and bent hedges. These late storms were harder to bear than the deep freeze of January; often on a spring night we were awakened by the groaning and cracking of limbs and spent the following day shaking snow from branches in an effort to save our valued and scattered trees.

Summer brought with it ideal days, bright, warm, and sun-wrapped. Nights were cool and stars seemed close enough to pluck from the sky. If rain had been plentiful, the lawn at Willowcroft was a deep blue-green and the pastures flourished with their mixture of grass and weeds. In dry years, the plains and foothills turned brown by July, dust rose in the river and creek beds, and the earth began to crack in the fields. Paul's watering plan would become tight and intricate as he spent hours dragging hoses this way and that way across the crisping lawn. Cee would pick up her shovel and, clad in shorts and galoshes, plod into the four acres where she spent the time between chores digging ditches and building dams to irrigate the ground with precious water.

Irrigating was tolerable at best; not only was it hard work but it required political as well as physical maneuvering to capture a good "head." Once the big ditch was flowing above Willowcroft, the neighbors might appropriate the water for weeks. Sometimes Cee would rise in the morning to find her gushing ditches a mere trickle after someone had opened a floodgate and stolen her head. When the upper half of the four acres was being flooded, the horses were switched to the lower half and vice versa, but there were those frequent times when the bunch escaped to the wrong pasture and broke down all Cee's carefully constructed dams. Or there was the minor discomfort of stepping out in sandals to catch a horse and finding yourself ankle deep in mud—or of tripping over a water snake. In dry summers Cee fell exhausted into bed at 9:00 P.M., dreaming of rushing rivers and week-long mists of rain.

In fact, a good part of every summer was spent wishing for rain. Almost every afternoon plump dark clouds sailed over the crustlike edge of the Rockies and the rain did fall, somewhere. That it was raining in Littleton, however, did not mean that it was raining at Willowcroft, a mile west. Often you could see the line across the road where the rain stopped; you could turn into Willowcroft drenched and still raise dust puffs in the driveway.

And the clouds, black, arbitrary, wildborn from the mountains, were always full of fire. Perhaps because of its particular location in a river valley, Willowcroft often failed to attract rain but beckoned lightning like a steel rod. As the clouds swelled and grumbled, Cee would become more and more nervous, wondering if she should get the horses in, for the salt on their wet hides was a natural invitation to a bolt of electricity. The darkest, loudest, and most sizzling clouds were those filled with hail. The horses sometimes would run terrified before a sheet of hail sweeping across the pasture until they were caught at the fence and pelted raw by ice.

One afternoon we were sitting on the front porch when it suddenly turned dark outside, the temperature dropped, and the wind began to blow. In the front pasture a pair of donkeys and their foals took shelter under the crab-apple tree while I headed upstairs to close Nana's windows. As I entered her bedroom, the house glowed with light and shook with a deafening crack of sound—I half expected it to split apart like the house of Usher. Then I heard my mother shout and the porch door slam and from a window I saw her run across the lawn toward the pasture. Beside the fence lay a donkey and foal, the mother motionless, the foal's hind legs still twitching. The second donkey was still standing under the tree, her long ears sagging, her foal safe beside her.

I rushed downstairs and yelled to Cee to come back, but she squeezed through the fence and bent over the dying donkeys. As she did there was another huge crack, and lightning stabbed from the clouds into the pasture behind the house. Cee darted in that direction while Nana and I stood on the porch and called in vain, not daring to venture into the inferno. When Cee returned we were in tears and so was she— the first mare she had ever rescued from the killers had been struck, leaving her four-month-old foal an orphan. It had taken Cee only a second to see that the mare was dead, and between one flash and boom and the next, she had driven the rest of the horses into the barn. In ten minutes we were able to count the seconds between the jagged streaks of lightning and the thunder that followed; in thirty minutes the sun was shining blandly on the wet, uplifted grass and on the two donkeys and the mare that lay with stiffened limbs, already beginning to bloat with death. It was a brilliant afternoon as I recall, smelling of rain, earth, rekindled growth.

There were other times when lightning grounded at Willowcroft—I was once startled from sleep as it crackled along the fuse box outside my window—and we learned to dread the thunderheads while welcoming the rain. But there were also years when water was too plentiful. Sometimes, especially after a dry spell, a storm would rage in the mountains, and, unable to absorb the overflow, creeks would cascade out of the canyons into the foothills and plains, picking up volume and power as they moved along. A flash flood could knock cars from the road, carry cattle from the fields, flatten fences, and destroy anything in its path.

Years ago, when we were still living at our first farm outside of Littleton, we saw a wall of water after a severe mountain storm hurtling down a creek that normally trickled through our pasture. Stopping only to pull on her rubbers, Cee rushed out to rescue the horses that were all standing on a little island in the middle of the stream. She managed to shoo them off, but they separated as the flood hit, and I, who had followed my mother, found myself trying to hang on to a screaming mare as her colt and Cee screamed back from the other side of a churning river. My mother was in water to her hips and the current threatened to tear her legs from under her any minute; there was no way across. Leaving the colt to its distress, Cee walked three miles to the nearest road, where Paul picked her up in the car. When she finally got home it was dark and she was wet, cold, and smelled slightly of the skunk she had nearly stepped on. All night the air reeled with the frantic calls of horses. Not until late morning did the water recede enough to allow a very hungry colt a joyous reunion with its distraught dam.

It was the summer of 1965, however, that will be remembered for floods, not only at Willowcroft but all over Arapahoe County. During the previous winter snow had piled high in the mountains, assuring prosperity for all the regional ski resorts. The snow kept coming until late spring, and when it did begin to melt the days were cool enough to keep the moisture in the earth. Streams rose and knocked against their banks like captured animals. Then on June 7 it began to rain, and rain came down day after day until the Platte River, which passed Willowcroft half a mile to the east, was so swollen and turbulent it looked as if it were laboring with some monstrous birth.

On the morning of June 14 the rain was falling at the rate of four inches an hour. The Platte flowed from south to north, parallel with the mountains. When tornadoes were reported in Monument, fifty miles south of Littleton, the family began to listen closely to the radio. At 3:30 P.M. a flash flood was reported in Plum Creek near Castle Rock thirty miles to the south; cresting as Plum Creek merged with the Platte, the flood was calculated to hit Littleton about 8:00 P.M. At 4:00 P.M. police cruisers with blowhorns ordering everybody out began to move up and down the road leading from Willowcroft east into Littleton. At 5:00 P.M. the Platte spilled over its banks, while huge uprooted trees and debris from upstream swirled and battered against the local bridge. Paul drove home from Littleton at 5:30—one of the last cars over the bridge.

Evacuating the animal and human population at Willowcroft was no small matter. After the first reports the phone jangled constantly with people offering help, supplies, and horse trailers. A friend of Cee's, Mary Wolverton, came straight from a cocktail party dressed in her finery and high heels, never dreaming she would not get home for two days. Another friend began hauling horses out in her trailer. But it was soon evident that thirty or more horses could not be moved off the place before the crest was due to hit. According to calculations, it would be almost twenty feet high by that time and would spread half a mile. At its highest point, Willowcroft was twenty-five feet above the level of the riverbed; if the figures were correct, the water would cover the lower pasture and perhaps touch the red barn, but the Big Building and the house would remain dry.

Cee moved most of the horses to the apple orchard behind the house. Just to be on the safe side she sent Paul to inform Nana, who was in bed with a bad cold, that she, also, would have to be moved.

Nana pulled her turquoise coverlet up to her chin when Paul entered her bedroom.

"Muddie," he said as gently as possible, "Cynthia is so worried about you that it would help if you consented to be evacuated. Mary Wolverton is here and she'll drive you up to high ground on the land to the west of here."

"Oh, I can't," protested Nana, who ached in every bone of her body. "I don't care what happens to me." But when she saw Paul's face she reconsidered. "Oh, all right. If Cynthia's that worried." A few minutes later, clad in nightgown, kimono, and satin slippers, Nana climbed in the truck with Mary, who had just finished loading Cee's best stallion and mare in the trailer. Then off they drove toward the highest hill west, where they remained until after the crest of the flood had passed. (Later Mary confessed she was feeling no pain after the cocktail party and that carrying on a proper conversation with a grandmother in her eighties was a far greater challenge than loading a skittish stallion.)

In the meantime, in spite of the sheriff's order to leave the premises, the family had decided to retreat no farther than Nana's vacated apartment on the second floor. From the porch roof they would be able to see the crest as it approached. In the housing development across the road people were frantically loading cars and U-Hauls with their possessions and trooping out in rows. Cee thought the only things worth saving were her animals, and soon she, dogs, cats, and Sherman were all comfortably installed in Nana's rooms. Paul found it easier to save nothing at all. He did, however, make sure to carry a can of peanuts upstairs with him. Bruce, on the other hand, was impressed enough with the situation to realize that he would need a few essentials to start life anew after the flood. First he parked his car in a friend's yard to the west, but after deciding the ground was too low, he ran it up the hill, where he left it in the company of Nana, Mary, and the horses. To make sure it was safe he made several excursions up and down before returning to the disaster area to retrieve the rest of his things. These consisted of every clean shirt he could find, which he carefully carried upstairs. Had the family been stripped of all they owned, they might have gone without food or water, but at least they all would have started out again in freshly laundered shirts.

Bruce's last mission was accomplished with little time to spare; already the rain-laden night was moving in. The horses had been restless for hours. Now they began to snort loudly and gallop in circles around the apple orchard, their nostrils flared and their tails furled over their backs. Every few minutes they would stop in a group and face the south. Hushed and waiting, Cee, Paul, and Bruce stood on Nana's porch. Then they heard what the horses had heard before them, a low almost subterranean rumble. Quickly the noise crescendoed to the volume of a freight train, then grew louder and louder until the roar of black water, foam, and swirling timbers seemed like a rocket launching. At the edge of the orchard telephone poles began to sway and crack and lines snapped like whips above the heads of the frantic horses.

"My God!" Bruce shouted. "Look!"

Rushing into view was a thick dark wall of water, on top of which, like a grotesquely misplaced crown, bobbed a recently built $60,000 house. When the house hit the local bridge, the old structure shuddered and swayed but miraculously held. For the next ten miles, all the way from Littleton northward to Denver, the newer bridges were wiped out.

As soon as the crest had passed the family raced down from Nana's porch to survey the damage. Mary and company returned in the truck. Calculations proved correct: the water had swamped the barnyard next door, torn down the lower-pasture fence, and spilled into the saucer-shaped corral beside the red barn. It rose no farther. Later the pond was used by Samson and Delilah, the Chinese geese. The river was still churning, however, and there were vague reports of a second crest coming which the family decided to ignore. At 2:30 A.M., thoroughly exhausted, they went to bed, only to be awakened an hour later by the barking of the sheriff's horn ordering complete evacuation; this time a major dam had broken.

"Absolutely not," declared Nana when Cee informed her she would have to be taken up the hill again. "If I'm going to be washed downstream in my bed, so be it."

"But, Mother—" Then Cee gave up. Clutching Sherman in her arms, she retreated from Nana's bedroom to her sitting room, where she found Bruce blinking fearfully over a new armload of shirts and Paul dozing in a chair. Fortunately the last alarm was only that, and all that was lost was a good night's sleep.

Perhaps the worst part for those who experience a natural disaster is not the moment of crisis itself but what is left in its wake. The next morning was cold and gray and threatening more rain. Power lines were down; electricity and phones were dead; what water remained in the taps was unfit to drink. Although the local bridge was still standing, congestion was so bad no one could cross unless he had a special permit from the National Guard. Like a silver fleet the entire trailer court on the east bank of the Platte had sailed majestically across the road; what were once fields were now junkyards or pools in which floated cars, uprooted trees, house gables, and steel girders, not to mention smaller appliances such as stoves, refrigerators, and washing machines.

If help were coming it would have to come from the west side of the river. The family did not have to wait long. Friends arrived with camping stove, kerosene, food, and buckets of fresh water. Mary volunteered to cook. After several hours her brother managed to get across the river and they began the slow job of transporting Cee's horses to a farm near the mountains. Since the only communication with the outside world was by transistor radio, friends on the Denver side of the river were relieved to hear Pete Smythe, who had crossed the bridge on foot to check, announce on radio that everything was all right at the Wolfs'. Eolis, who had spent a dry but anxious night at her home in Denver, was especially relieved. In the East Craig and I first heard about the Littleton flood on a news broadcast and, unable to reach Willowcroft, phoned Eolis, who assured us the place was still standing. The enforced blackout was too much for Bruce, who finally hiked across the bridge to Littleton to telephone his girl. At the end of three days without phone or electricity Cee had lost five pounds and her temper many times and Paul had become an expert at mixing drinks without ice. As for Nana, she announced that as soon as the bridge was repaired she was moving in town to the Park Lane Hotel. "I've had enough of living like an aborigine," she declared.

While many people lost possessions in the flood, no human lives were lost. It was different with the animals. Cattle, sheep, and horses were sucked from fields miles upstream, and the river became a grisly maelstrom of dead and wounded livestock. Surviving animals ran loose all over the countryside. Eleven Angus cattle, one red cow, six horses, including two Thoroughbreds from a nearby racetrack and a Shetland stallion, all floated into our lower pasture after the crest had passed. Still in her cocktail dress, Mary had waded up to her shoulders trying to rescue the stallion, who immediately plunged back into the raging torrent in pursuit of a Thoroughbred filly caught in loose strands of barbed wire. Mary managed to untangle her, but the filly was too weak to buck the current and the river snatched her away until at last it deposited her in a clump of cattails farther downstream. Her legs were severed to the bone. In the meantime both the stud and Mary had scrambled to dry ground and headed for the house. It was then that Mary borrowed a pair of Paul's pants and settled down for an indefinite stay while the stud, eluding all attempts at capture, spent the rest of the night tormenting our remaining stallions and herding the exhausted, half-crazy mares. Not until late the next day was Willowcroft relieved of its unwelcome visitor when two men roped him and carted him off.

Looking over her pasture full of strays the morning after, Cee said she'd keep them a week, then call the sheriff. Most pople turned up to claim their scattered livestock, while others brought their horses by to see if they could stable them in the only dry barn around. Cee was glad enough to get rid of her unexpected company, except for the red cow, which caught her eye and which she finally bought for $100. At the racetrack to the north the barns had been opened wide as the flood approached and most of the horses turned loose. Afterward dead horses were found everywhere, even floating inside a nearby bowling alley. Those that survived were so cut by wire and debris and so infected by sand in their cuts that the veterinarians were forced to work around the clock simply to destroy the animals; they did not even attempt to save them. The only race-horses that escaped unscathed were those that were led into the grandstand and held. "Next time a flood hits I'll tie everything in the barn and not budge," insisted Cee.

Tales are still told about the flood of 1965, when many of the animals performed more intelligently and heroically than the people. There was the Arabian stallion that broke through two fences, rounded up his mares, and drove them safely to high ground. On the other hand, one old mare panicked and was followed by her entire herd into the river and to death. The response of the animals was instinctive, simply to live or to die. People's response to the flood was not only more sophisticated but at times blatantly materialistic. One man gathered up all the wandering cattle and horses he could find and charged their owners $40 a head to get them back. Looters raided the evacuated trailer court even before the crest of the river carried it off; a woman who had rushed her ailing child to the Littleton Clinic returned briefly to find that someone had stolen her stove and washing machine.

Yet there were other stories, neither especially heroic nor deplorable, but small stories of endurance, humor, and blind refusal to recognize the worst. Almost simultaneously with the looting, people began to clean up and rebuild. Not many moved away. Instead, mud was shoveled from basements, water-logged furniture was set in the sun to dry, new crops and lawns and gardens planted. Scattered possessions were located and taken home. One man and his wife walked a mile downriver from their home in search of a prized silver chest which they spotted bobbing around in our lower pasture. Accompanied by Paul they waded out to retrieve it, but when the wife opened a drawer, instead of knives and forks, half a dozen water snakes poured out, much to her horror and the men's delight.

Within a year new trailers were lined up where the old ones had been and a restaurant which had been completely flattened had reopened only a few hundred yards upstream. Flood-control bills were pushed through the state legislature and hundreds of acres condemned for a dam site. Four years later was another wet year and the dam was still on paper. The river rose and began to groan and people wondered if they were crazy, but they stayed, moved their furniture upstairs, tied their horses in the barn. Once again the restaurant and trailer court were inundated; once again they were rebuilt. Roots were too deep and lives were too much like the river—it might rise and fall, twist and toss in its bed, but it would move on, essentially unchanged, down to an open sea.

13

Smooth Landing

I WAS JOLTED out of a semidream state by the captain's voice on the intercom announcing our approach to Denver. Feeling my anxiety return, I pressed my forehead against the cold double glass of the window. We had dropped low enough to see the long upward sweep of the great plains that composed most of eastern Colorado, and farther on, the belt of haze that marked the front range of the Rockies. In a few minutes the first jagged peaks thrust themselves from the haze; one, still topped with snow, I recognized as Mount Evans. Soon tiny, naked-looking houses dotted the prairie, and as we began to circle, I caught a glimpse of the ragged zigzag of cottonwoods along the Platte River, no more than a muddy trickle from the air. Another dry year, I could tell.

Denver itself appeared below me, sprawling untidily as if someone had dropped it out of a bag and forgotten to pick it up. In the fifties when I was growing up on its outskirts, it had been a comfortable town, a neat cross-hatching of streets at the base of the Rockies, with buildings not much higher than the Brown Palace Hotel. During the next decade it slowly but perceptibly had begun to crawl off in all directions. In recent years a dense, sulfurous cloud floated over the city each day, shutting out the sky. Now, as we circled, the cloud seemed longer and lower than the summer before, touching the glassy tops of high-rise buildings and stretching south from Denver almost as far as Littleton. The plane tilted and plunged suddenly into the swirling vapor. I closed my eyes as we descended.

"Hey, Alice, over here." Bruce had been sent to fetch me at the airport. His face was tanned, his nose distinctly red. We quickly bumped cheeks.

"How's Mum?" I asked anxiously. "Why didn't she come to meet me?"

"She's got an ad in the paper. She's been sitting by the phone for a week. Dad was coming but some guy dropped by to talk politics just as we were leaving."

"Do you mean she's really trying to sell the horses? I can't believe—"

"Are you kidding? She picked up a team of Missouri mules somewhere and she wants to trade them for something—like a herd of ponies, maybe."

"Then she's just as bad as ever," I said happily—then automatically slipped back into my old role as protester against such excesses. "She should cut down."

"Yeah. There's not an empty stall in the barn."

"How many horses do you have there?"

Bruce gave me a flash of brown eyes. "Five or six, maybe. She doesn't have to worry about them. I take care of them myself."

I decided to change the subject. "How's Dad?"

"Busy. He's running for reelection in the fall."

I groaned. "I thought he said he was going to retire

this time." Again this year I would see very little of my father.

"How—?" I began again but stopped. What I really wanted to know I had to find out for myself. What was it like without Nana? How much had Willowcroft changed since her death? I was oddly reluctant to follow my brother from the airport to the parking lot where he stood squinting at the rows of cars, searching for his own.

As we drove south toward Littleton along the Platte, Bruce rambled on about his new job with a real estate firm and the four ranches he'd sold during the year. Nervously I stared at block after block of shopping centers and filling stations that now linked Denver to Littleton.

"In twenty years there'll be one big city stretching from here to Colorado Springs," Bruce predicted, as if reading my mind. I had to agree. Denver was becoming too big, too hungry and thirsty for the land. I wondered what would happen if there was a major drought some year.

Though it was still June, it was dry and very hot, the sun burning out of a flat blue sky with that intensity peculiar to the West, where there is little shade to dilute its rays. The grass was withered, the color of straw. Not until we turned west on the road to Willowcroft did I have my first real look at the mountains, blue-green in the afternoon, snow crowning many of the peaks along the continental divide.

In a few minutes we were home. It surprised, then reassured me to see that the old stone house looked the same as ever, though the willows shading the front porch were fuller and the lilac hedge was badly in need of a trim. My father, dressed in baggy blue bermudas, was lugging a hose across the lawn. As Bruce eased over the bump in the driveway half a dozen dogs rushed from the house, followed by Cee clad in shorts and galoshes, a shovel over her shoulder. She was already tanned a deep brown.

Greeting my parents over the barking while defending my stockings from dozens of canine toenails took some effort, but I succeeded at last and began to count heads. Only two shepherds were familiar from the summer before; the rest of the dogs were new. I looked at my mother.

"Well, Mum, have you been camping at the Dumb Friends League lately?"

Her eyes, large and full of gold flecks, turned innocently toward me. "Not since May," she admitted, smiling. "I've got something else to show you. Just a minute."

"Not another animal," I protested in Nana's tone of voice. But I couldn't help laughing as Cee rushed to the laundry room off the back porch. She returned at once with a small brown creature perched on her shoulder, its tail looped around her arm.

"This is Harry," she announced proudly.

"Oh, for heaven's sake. Wouldn't you know you'd end up with a monkey."

"A woolly monkey," corrected Cee. "They're quite rare, you know. I found him at a pet store and I couldn't resist. He gets along fine with Sherman and Samantha."

Harry grabbed a handful of hair and climbed to the top of Cee's head, where he sat gazing at me with round, close-set eyes.

"She thought you'd like to keep him in your room for company since Craig's not here," said Paul. He winked and we all laughed. Definitely I was home.

The next morning, unable to sleep through the din of animal voices, I made my way to the barn before breakfast. Dust rose from the large corral, clearing to reveal Bruce engaged in a fierce tug-of-war with a month-old colt. The colt pulled against its new halter and rope with all its young strength, forelegs extended until its chest almost touched the ground, rump high in the air. Its eyes bulged, sweat darkened its neck, its nostrils fanned like pink, translucent flowers. Nearby stood its mother, wearing the halter which was the seal of her domesticity. Now and then she flicked her ears toward her silent, resisting youngster. Once she had fought like that and lost. The colt would lose also—it was strong, but no match for Bruce's experience.

I entered the Big Building just as Cee came through the other end carrying a large basket of wood shavings. Unobserved, I stood in the shadows a moment, watching her closely. Her hair was lighter, almost white, her face sharply lined as she moved hurriedly from stall to stall spreading shavings. With the third basketload she began to slow down. She was puffing heavily but she did not stop to rest; instead, she suddenly speeded up again as if she recalled some hypothetical deadline—the winged chariot at her back. I took a few steps into the stable and something swooped chittering from the rafters—Harry. I ducked too late; the next thing I knew he was on my head, one hand clutching a fistful of hair, the other pressed firmly across my mouth. The more I struggled to dislodge him the harder he pulled and the louder he screeched. Cee stopped in her tracks and laughed.

"Get him off!" I pleaded.

"He just wants to get acquainted."

"I don't want to get acquainted with a monkey. Yuck." I wiped my mouth as Harry leaped to the safety of Cee's shoulder.

"Wait," she said, "I've got something I know you'll like." Opening the door of the last stall, she led out a gray mare not much larger than a pony which she cross-tied in the aisle. The mare was a pretty thing, with straight, clean legs, large eyes, and a refined head. I stroked her face, my fingers lingering on the velvety patch of skin just above her nose. It palpitated delicately with her breathing.

"She's my new trail horse," said Cee.

"Your what?"

"Didn't I write you? I've taken up competitive trail riding. A whole bunch of us have."

"Where do you ride?"

"Everywhere. The last time was at the foot of Mount Evans, about seventy miles. It was up and down all the way, really rough. I didn't win anything, but the mare was amazing the way she held up. She scrambled through the timber better than the big horses. She never turned a hair."

"What about you?"

Cee glanced at me quickly. "Don't worry, I can take care of myself." I had the feeling that her answer had been rehearsed.

Later that morning after Paul and Bruce had left for work I found myself alone in the kitchen with Eolis. Over the years I had noticed that my mother had come to depend upon Eolis almost as much as my grandmother. Her tranquilizer, Cee called her. Now I was glad to see that Eolis came each day as ever, making sure the front of the house was kept bright and airy and that Sherman got his exercise and cuddling.

"How has it been since Nana died?" I asked hesitantly during the course of our conversation.

Eolis looked up from the potatoes she was peeling in the sink. "Mrs. Wolf didn't know what to do with herself right afterward. It was a hard winter for her. She'd been so used to having your grandmother—" She paused, trying to choose her words carefully. "Well, you know she couldn't really get away from Willowcroft for so many years. The animals held her down but your grandmother did too. Mrs. Wolf just didn't feel right leaving her. This spring she started the trail rides."

I frowned. "What do you think of that? Aren't they awfully long and hard? All the people she rides with are younger. I think she's pushing herself."

Eolis dried her hands on a towel. "Yes," she answered slowly, "I guess she is. But I guess she has her reasons. No one's likely to make her stop."

Promptly at one o'clock Cee reported for lunch. We ate in the kitchen, on the worn yellow table which Eolis had carefully laid with Nana's good silver. I was amused and glad that the old habits had survived. My mother and Eolis discussed the market list, the dogs, arrangements for the end of the week when Cee expected to leave with two friends for a two-day ride in the mountains.

"You don't mind me going, Alice?" she asked apologetically. "I know you just got here, but we've been planning it for ages. You can come along if you want. We'll have Dottie's camper and Peg is going to cook. It should be lots of fun."

"What about chores?"

"Bruce'll take care of the horses and Paul the dogs when Eolis isn't here. Why don't you come along?"

"No thanks. I couldn't ride ten miles at this point, let alone fifty. Don't you think . . ." I started to admonish her as tactfully as possible that people approaching seventy were damned fools to go galloping all over the countryside on competitive trail rides. Then I stopped. I remembered what she had said to me long ago before I left for college. I wouldn't pretend to hang on to her. She needed to make up for lost time.

That afternoon Cee retired to the barn to telephone while I wandered restlessly about the quiet house. I had been accustomed to spending these hours with Nana, and it felt strange not to be sitting with her on the porch or in her room. On my way upstairs I hesitated on the landing outside her door. Then gently I turned the knob and entered. Everything was in its place, the curtains open, the canopy bed neatly made as if she had only stepped out for a few hours. A book lay on her table by her chair in the sitting room and, beside it, her reading glasses. I could almost hear her say, "Sit down, dear, and tell me what you've been doing." Then for the next hour or two we would talk and all the time she'd be nodding her white head and gesturing with her fine, old hands as the light deepened in the window behind her.

I turned to her writing desk, seeking something I wasn't certain of myself. A carved sea gull with outstretched wings looked as if it were about to sail from the top of the desk, while inside, in one of the cubby-holes, another sea gull perched on one leg. Softly I swished the little drawers in and out, their mahogany surface smooth and cool to my touch. In one was a dried-up bottle of ink, in another a few old pencil stubs. The last contained a packet of letters I recognized immediately, letters Nana had written to me at college. I thought I'd lost them a long time ago. I closed the drawer with a click and retreated downstairs to the front porch, the letters in my hand.

They all began in the same way, with my grandmother apologizing for being such a poor correspondent. I read them slowly, puzzling out Nana's spidery handwriting, beautifully even but almost illegible, recalling with pleasure the forgotten words. From time to time she would plead with me to try to be happy at school; eventually it would be worth the price of homesickness, she assured me. Then she would go on to tell about life at Willowcroft, my mother's adventures with the horses, my father's campaigning, her own mock horror at the ever-increasing company of animals. "Cynthia is absolutely incorrigible," she wrote, "but I love her anyway." I could imagine the impatient shake of her head, her helpless smile even as she set down her pen. Scold, humor, remonstrate as she would with her daughter, her tone was finally one of acceptance. Through every word ran a fine but indestructible strand of love.

"I hope someday you'll write a saga on your mother," the last letter in Nana's packet began. Then she proceeded to tell me in detail Cee's latest encounter with one of the menagerie.

When I had finished I sat a long time looking up

through the shimmering leaves of the cottonwood tree to the west of the porch. Beyond the tree the mountains were turning lavender in the late afternoon. It occurred to me that I had never needed to wonder what would happen when Nana died. For there never was a question. We were still of one piece, still bound, the past living in the present and going on.

I stretched and smiled as I heard dogs yapping and Cee's footsteps in the gravel. Chores must be over.

14

Catching Up

CLANG. The iron butt bar hits the side of the trailer like
a hammer on an anvil—hoofs thud, backing out. In the
house upstairs I open the door to the porch roof in time
to see my mother, leading something with an angular
rump and longish ears, disappear behind the lilac hedge.
The mist still hovers above the pasture, and as I watch,
the sun spreads slowly across the pink wall of the Big
Building, just visible through a screen of leaves. Somewhere east of the barn what begins as a whinney turns
abruptly into a series of wheezing grunts, answered in
kind nearby. My mother failed to mention last night
that she planned an early morning expedition. But I
don't need to guess what Cee has hauled back to Willowcroft.

   I'm also back for an annual visit. More than ten
years have passed since I sat on the front porch reading Nana's letters; now I'm installed in her room and
spend my nights under the pleated turquoise canopy
of her bed. In Nana's adjacent sitting room my young
daughter, Amanda, is still asleep on a cot. Nothing
much has changed: the seagulls on the wall, the desk
full of cubby holes, the antique walnut table on which

207

sits an enameled radio, no longer working. Minnie the mule's latest ribbon, a blue, is draped over the top. Across the road outside a backhoe goes to work, its beeb beeb mingling with the honking of Canada geese overhead. The scent of lilacs mixes with the smell of manure.

Yesterday's quick inspection of the barn revealed the same lead ropes as last year snapped on the side of a stall, the hose and brigade of buckets, the two wheelbarrows, the neat line of shovels and brooms, the horse vacuum cleaner and, for all I know, the same fly-studded flypaper. Alfalfa, sawdust. The rooster, brilliantly feathered, perched on the rafters. "I raised him," said Cee proudly. "He's the last of the bunch. Racoons got the rest." Willowcroft appears to be functioning much as it did a decade ago. Or is this only what I want to believe?

One of the first things I noticed this trip was that the Denver telephone book seemed nearly equal in size to the Manhattan directory. Littleton claims two of its own - one white, one yellow. The suburban sprawl underway in the fifties has filled the countryside; once open farmland has sprouted developments and shopping centers reaching to the foothills. In between are arid rectangles, reverted to gopher holes and thistles, posted with large signs announcing commercial expansion. The racetrack has given way to condominiums. To the west of Willowcroft an office complex obscures the mountains; across Bowles to the north is a revitalized shopping center replacing an older one. Although a few of the cottonwoods along Bowles Avenue still stand, the traffic, during rush hour, backs up to the Platte River Bridge. The road is now being widened.

At the northwest corner of the front pasture, a

traffic light allows Cee to turn her truck and four horse trailer from the lane into Bowles, the stream of vehicles parting on either side of her like water around a log. Almost every morning except Monday, which is marketing morning, she is on her way to Chatfield, a 2,000 acre state park five miles to the south created when the Chatfield Dam was built in the 1970s to control floods like the one that destroyed parts of Littleton in 1965. Here Cee can ride nearly 15 miles over open land and through woods where the dammed up Platte meanders in new channels every spring. Sailboats skim across the main lake, and a host of wildlife breed in the rushes surrounding pools of backwater: blue herons and Canada geese, cormorants, a variety of ducks, and colonies of beaver which divert the water and wreak havoc with the riding trails. Cee has sat many a horse shying at a mule deer or the sudden swoop of an owl startled from a tree overhead.

To make a loop back to the trailer, the river has to be crossed; Cee forces her horse belly deep into the current at every opprotunity. "Good training," she assures me. I was riding with her and friends one spring when the river was just past flood stage. There was a short debate whether to cross or not—the next thing I knew Cee was up to her thighs with the others right behind. I realized that they were all drifting swiftly downstream, then Cee's horse gained a foothold and scrambled up the bank on the far side of the river. I stood on the other bank with my heart in my mouth and my horse dancing nervously, neither of us wanting to take the plunge. If I turned around, my pride was at stake - and I was sure to get lost. The others had pulled themselves out somewhat further downstream than they'd intended.

"Come on Alice, if I can do it, so can you," shouted my mother, secure on the opposite side. I slammed my heels into my mare's sides and the water hit us with a cold shock. For a few seconds I could feel her chest push against the current, her hoofs sliding and clinking over the slippery rocks on the bottom, then the clatter ceased as she began to swim and the current carried us further and further from the line of witnesses on shore. A few hundred yards downstream the river slackened and my mare found the bottom and plunged to dry ground. As I stood trying to collect my wits, Cee breezed by me, water dripping from her saddle cinch. "Now that wasn't so bad, was it?" she called over her shoulder. Nevertheless, I noticed she rode home by way of a bridge.

Like the Phipps ranch, Chatfield has a respectable coyote population, and like the rest of the animals they manage to coexist with the people who come to camp, fish and use the trails. If Cee drops a glove, a coyote will chew it up; if she brings a dog with her, a coyote will chase it. She now leaves her dogs at home when she rides. The mountains, viewed through a snarl of high tension wires, seem closer here than at the ranch. But if man and nature must make compromises, Chatfield is one of the better ones.

It took an impromptu history lesson to make us realize the transformations that have taken place at Willowcroft in the last 120 years. One day Cee and Paul received a surprise visit from Ray Bowles, grandson of Joseph Wesley Bowles who built the main house at Willowcroft in the 1860s. His grandfather, Bowles said, a buffalo hunter, migrated west over the Kansas Territory of which Colorado was a part. In 1859, when gold was discovered in the Pikes Peak region, Joseph Bowles headed for what is now Gilpin County, becoming its first sheriff while he was engaged in mining the Burroughs lode. In the fall of 1862 he purchased a homestead claim near the present town of Littleton.

At age 21 Joseph Bowles had managed to accumulate a sizable chunk of territory, some 5,000 acres of land stretching from the Platte River to the mountains, on which he built his manor house, later named Willowcroft, and the first complete irrigation system in the Colorado Territory. Today the house, one of three ranch houses, is registered as an historic landmark with the state of Colorado. The other original building on the place, according to Ray Bowles, was a smokehouse and cellar for potatoes and apples, which my mother later converted to a stallion shelter, "Abou's House."

Indians and buffalo were so numerous in the 1860s that the enterprising Joseph Bowles invented a heavy duty barbed wire to keep the buffalo (if not the Indians) off his hay fields. We also learned that the green pond in the pony corral where Samson and Delilah used to swim was once the Bowles family fishing pond in which they caught their Friday night supper.

Of the original acreage today, Willowcroft claims just ten, and the pond has shrunk to a noxious puddle that disappears entirely in a dry year. The crabapple trees, planted by Nana and David, tower above the railing on the second story porch, but the willows that once gave the place its name have not fared well, and only a stump with a few branches remains on the front lawn, thick and luxurious thanks to the efforts of Louise who has taken over the gardening and Paul's network of hoses. From a pole near the house, two faded flags fly bravely, one representing the U.S., the other, a state that did not even exist when Joseph Bowles first made his way to the Platte River. In the 1980s, Willowcroft is an anomaly, a tiny rural island teeming with animal life in the midst of a paved and mechanized landscape. Beyond the bleating and braying can be heard the clash of traffic, the urgent shriek of sirens that set all the dogs on the place to howling.

No longer inhabited by Sherman, Samantha and company, the laundry room has been usurped by a half dozen or more raggedy little dogs who are bedded down each night on select sheets from *The Wall Street Journal.* Sherman, who ate nothing but peanut butter in his old age, perished of it. Samantha escaped through the dog door when Cee was away and disappeared, but Amy returned from her numerous forays in the Willowcroft wilds to die, at age 13, in Cee's lap. Missing but not missed from its spot by the lilac hedge is Bruce's four-horse trailer, the "Yellow Submarine," a relic of the days Bruce dreamed of championships and packed himself and entourage off to the nearest horseshow. Bruce now judges horseshows instead of participating in them, an avocation that takes him all over the United States, and to such exotic places as Brazil and Australia. Still, Cee claims she has gone further on the back of a horse than her son has gone in an airplane.

In 1982 Paul retired from his 21 year stint as Arapahoe County Treasurer. He was named Citizen of the Year, received a dinner in his honor, a gold watch, and much time. The change was something of a shock, and without an office to go to, Paul, who is still "catching up" with a lifetime of unfinished business, sometimes gets off with a slower than usual start. "I shouldn't have washed my hair this morning," he muses. "All my energy drained out."

Still, the day-to-day changes at Willowcroft are gentle ones, and I am most aware of what is familiar and routine. Cee's schedule remains the same; chores begin at 6:00 a.m., breakfast at 8:00; Eolis arrives at 9:00; riding at 10:00; lunch, a sandwich and chips in the kitchen, is dispatched with as soon as Cee returns from her ride. Pausing to glance at a soap opera flickering from a tiny TV on top of a kitchen cabinet, Cee and Eolis discuss the problems of the day. As in the past, Eolis makes sure that there aren't too many false starts, that Cee is pointed toward the market and Paul makes a stab at the heap of papers on his desk. One morning Eolis arrived in time to catch Cee's recently purchased truck as it went for a solitary spin across the front lawn; not used to an automatic transmission, Cee had shifted into drive instead of park, hopped out and marched into the house without a backward glance. With Eolis in pursuit, the truck plowed through the forsythia bushes and was about to garland itself with the front pasture fence when she made a final sprint and grabbed the emergency brake. Eolis has proved herself adept with a set of jumper cables, rushing to the rescue when Cee stalled the truck miles from Willowcroft. With characteristic diplomacy, she has retrieved lost checks from the pile on Paul's desk and conducted a systematic search for his dentures. Ever sympathetic, Eolis has remained the calm center of many a Willowcroft storm.

Cee hasn't mellowed much; if anything, her particular likes and dislikes have become more pronounced. Her hair is as white as Nana's and her frame is slight, but she's as tough as a fence post and stubborn as ever, though it takes her a little longer to throw a 30 pound saddle on her horse. Housework is the anathema it's always been; of her vacuum cleaner she observed, "I don't think there's an instrument alive that can infuriate me more. It's so stupid it goes out of its way to bug me. If it's not stubbing its nose on every chair it's flipping itself over and lying helplessly on its back, with me in a rage. I'll use a broom every time I can in spite of the fact it blows hairs all over hell." The barn, of course, is meticulously swept every morning.

Cooking for Cee is still in the category of an afterthought - or no thought at all. "Today," she wrote, "I put seven eggs on the stove on full and then walked out of the kitchen and became so drowsy I went over to the swing (on the front porch) and conked out a few minutes. When I awakened I smelled the most ghastly odor. Do you know those damn eggs had frizzled so hard they exploded all over the kitchen I'd just mopped? I don't know why things like that happen to me."

Although the animal population at Willowcroft has a yearly turnover, it is constant. There are a dozen dogs in the kitchen and more outside. The horse count dwindles or expands according to Cee's whims. She is no longer looking for the perfect horse, just one with a fast walk, a smooth trot, and a pulse and respiration of 48 and 24. Competitive trail riding has given her ample time for experimentation; she has gone through a succession of breeds - Passo Finos, Tennessee Walkers, Missouri Foxtrotters, American Mustangs - before returning to a string of lean and laid back Arabs, happily wheeling and dealing one horse for the next. Her latest discovery wears a stripe down its back and sports a pair of ears as long as Cee's forearms.

Various fowls have joined the menagerie in the last few years; four geese and a mallard duck who thinks himself a goose patrol the Willowcroft premises, sleeping in the shade under Cee's truck and dunking periodically in the tepid waters of a plastic wading pool. Cee has always liked a good goose, but I carefully avoid this sinuous-necked tribe, as my memories of my encounter with Samson are rekindled. When I called Cee from New York one spring, she answered on the barn telephone, and I heard a chorus of crowing in the background. "Those are my banty roosters," she explained. "Ten and only two hens, worst luck." Cee became enamored of banties after Bruce, who envisioned himself making his fortune training trotting horses, bought a Standardbred mare and began to spend early mornings at the track. Next door he discovered a bunch of starving chickens and brought one home to his mother. More were to follow, "rescued" from a scruffy life of neglect. "There'll probably be headlines in the *Littleton Independent*: Paul Wolf Treasurer of Arapahoe County - Wife Found Guilty of Chicken Thievery," clucked Cee. Eggs began to appear in the Willowcroft mangers in various stages of abandonment, and it was my son Lex's job to collect them (avoiding the setting hens) during our summer visits. It took about ten banty eggs to make an omelet which, for obvious reasons, no one would eat.

For awhile, the little fowls flourished. "After four generations of inbreeding, I'm now getting white chickens out of black, otherwise they seem to have all their marbles," wrote Cee. But in spite of her good intentions, a number of Cee's chickens met untimely and often violent ends, drowning in water buckets or dispatched by her own dogs. She found herself surrogate mother to more than one chick, including one she installed in a cage in the back living room with a feather duster for companionship. "Chickadee is so sweet," she informed me. "It likes to be petted. I forgot I left it out and went to the barn and called it when I got back. It chirped and I traced its voice to the riding clothes closet where it was sitting on a boot. It's really too big for the cage and still sleeps under the duster. I can't bear to put it in the barn and have anything happen to it, but I can't have a full grown chicken in the house." A few weeks later Cee discovered Chickadee was a hen. "Her brother is learning to crow," she wrote, "while Chickadee is still snuggling under her duster. Paul hopes when Eolis shakes the mop out, Chickadee doesn't fall it the stew pot." Cee finally took the chicken to the barn where, predictably, one night it vanished down something's throat.

The most exotic creatures at Willowcroft are a flock of Barbado sheep, sleek brown with black faces and wild at heart. A miniature Zebu cow with six teats and half a hump has replaced the ubiquitous Jersey. On a hot August afternoon, Cee became the happy recipient of the little cow's husky calf, placed wetly in her arms after a well documented Cesarean section. The goats have disappeared, including big black Wilbur who spent all his time grazing with the horses. And Harry the monkey is gone, but not without leaving a most memorable mark on Willowcroft.

During his short but mischievous stay with Cee, Harry repeated Sherman's old tricks, climbing into visitors' cars, eating a fresh cake one day, prescription pills in someone's purse the next, whereupon he was given a dose of Ipecac and put to bed. During a picture taking session with the *Denver Post*, while Cee was being photographed at the barn shoveling manure, Harry was busy at the house devastating the kitchen. After polishing off the meringue on Eolis' cocoanut custard pie, he fled through the dog door and sprawled innocently in the sun outside. The *Post* photographer discovered him and requested that Harry pose by the newly erected sign in the driveway, "Keep Windows Closed, Monkey at Large." Harry, however, was not to be caught.

Shortly afterward he had a chance to perfect his social graces with another member of the simian set, a female named Bridget. Cee recounted the event in a long letter: "They (the White family) came around six with Bridget dressed in a fluffy pink and white romper looking very feminine. Harry was stark naked. She's a silver woolly and somewhat larger than he. Her skin and eyes are darker. She has a habit of rolling her tongue around her cheeks. Both monkeys eyed each other indifferently and Harry went off to play with their two children, and Bridget continued rolling her tongue around and clinging to Mrs. White. She thought it would be a good idea to undress her and let her and Harry play in the willow tree. Bridget ran to the top as branches cracked and broke. Harry stayed near the bottom.

"Since the monkeys weren't enjoying each other, the Whites decided to go home, but Bridget wouldn't budge - 8:00 p.m. came and there she sat at least 25 feet over our heads. They felt sure were we to squirt her with the hose she'd come down. She moved around and got thoroughly soaked but held her ground. Mrs. White took the children home for supper and bed while he stayed - 9:00, 10:00, and 11:00 came - there sat Bridget on the highest branch, a dark blurb against the light filled sky.

"At 12:00 I politely excused myself and went home to a very sleepless sleep. Mr. White went home for a bite to eat and brought back some blankets. I had to get up at 5:00 a.m. to get to a show at Adams County Fairgrounds. I looked out the window. Bridget was huddled asleep on her branch and the Whites were rolled up in their blankets at the foot of the tree while the ten and eleven year old kids were home alone. At 6:30 Mrs. White threatened Bridget with her going home; Bridget decided she'd go along too, as it just might be time for breakfast. The last I saw she was clinging to her "mother," stark naked, happily rolling her tongue her cheeks. Harry was just waking up. The Whites had nine boxers, so Bridget wasn't afraid of dogs. We decided she was in shock over Harry!"

After the publication of *Kinkajou*, Harry accompanied Cee to autograph parties. "Saturday I decided to tune up Harry for his appearances," wrote Cee. "First was a bath. Carefully I removed him from his cage to dunk him in the tub. He took one look, grabbed his cage with four hands and a tail and there was no way I could unpry him. I finally let him go back to his cage where I grabbed his hands and rushed him to the tub. He wrapped his tail around the pipe, let out loud oaths and settled into the water. I held his hands and washed with my free one. I never got his tail unpried to wash that. He liked being dried. When I went to put on his Pampers, they wouldn't fit. All his clothes were outgrown."

New clothes were found for Harry who impatiently endured the book signing sessions. Not half as fond of the public as they of him, Harry eventually grew grumpy. He took to biting people, first a miscellaneous boy, then

Marilyn, then Eolis, and finally Cee. Fearing reper-
cussions, she decided, at last, to send him to a new
home with a man experienced in monkey behavioral
problems whom she found through the Colorado Springs
Simian Society. "I feel as if I've lost my youngest child,"
mourned Cee.

But an animal never created a vacuum in Cee's life
without another to fill it. Soon after Harry's departure
brother David presented Cee with a white "weaner" pig.
Although she knew what was in store for her, my mother
never dreamed of refusing this gift from her eldest son.
"I think I'll teach her to lead before she gets too big,"
she wisely determined.

"Miss Piggy" got big all too quickly. After the pig
had, in Cee's words, rototilled the dog yard and escaped
to the field next door (it took three people to round her
up), Cee decided to build her a pen of her own. "I think
she's going to be an expensive pig," said Cee propheti-
cally. In three months she was the size of a German
Shepherd and eating as only a pig can eat. Besides grain
and hay every day she consumed a bucket full of table
scraps, everything, that is, except orange and grapefruit
rinds. She could squirt the juice of a cantaloupe three
feet by holding the whole fruit in her teeth and snapping
shut her jaws. Craig envisioned her as a side of bacon or
on a platter with apple in mouth, but when he made his
observations known to Cee, she cut him short.

"Don't say that about my pig. She loves me."

In spite of her small eyes, Piggy was intelligent and
meticulous about her housekeeping. Rarely did she soil
her shed, using the far corner of the pen for a bathroom.
In winter she piled dirt and straw in her house for a
warm nest; in summer she knocked it down again and

spent the hot part of the day outside in a mudhole Cee filled with a hose. She was never taught to lead, but she did learn to come when called from pasture where she was allowed to graze with the horses every afternoon. Unlike Wilbur, she didn't confuse herself with a horse, but she could snort and buck with the best of them, 800 pounds of ham as effortlessly airborn as a football player receiving a pass.

When it was time to put the porker to bed, Cee would bellow in her best hog calling voice, "Here Piggy, Piggy, Piggy," and then to all assembled, "Look out, here comes the pig!" Woe to any dog, horse or person in Piggy's path as she hurtled through the barn on a fast track to her grain. Once she was in the shed, she was bolted in, for it would take two strong men to push the door shut if Piggy decided she wanted out again.

It wasn't long before Willowcroft began to fill up with pink porcine artifacts: pig plates and mugs, stuffed pigs, pig notepaper, pig music boxes, given to Cee by admiring friends. One August day she returned from her ride to find a host of people ensconced on the front lawn. "Has Paul some damn Republican meeting and forgot to tell me?" she queried her riding companions. Sue and Peggy had been unusually dilatory that morning; in an attempt to detain the ever prompt Cee, Peggy had made Cee hold her horse while she sat in a convenient out-house at Chatfield for 20 minutes thumbing through a book and sizzling in the ninety degree heat. The "Repub-licans," vets Bill Howarth, Charlie Vail and 45 other friends of Cee's, gave a cheer and parted ranks when they saw her, revealing a life size cement pig with four piglets at the edge of the lawn, a weighty addition to the Willowcroft premises. It still stands where it was placed eight years ago. While Cee and friends celebrated, Miss Piggy was released from her pen to inspect this latest loving gift, whereupon she made a vain attempt to bite a hunk from its concrete hide.

"Some pig," she snorted.

15

Riding High

IF THERE'S been one consistent theme in Cee's life in the last ten years it's been Competitive Trail Riding. The rides, held from May through September, are an objective for Cee and her friends throughout the year, a reason to ride in bitter cold and high heat. They think nothing of trotting up the side of a mountain, sliding down 45 degree embankments, fording rivers or bushwacking through miles of downed timber all in the name of "conditioning." After each long climb, the rider leaps to the ground, takes her horse's pulse and times its respiration. My idea of a good ride is how many vistas or wildflowers it reveals; Cee's is how well it builds stamina. Cee's horse fulfills its potential as a competitive trail horse only when its heart slows down to 48 beats a minute, it barely breathes, its legs are as solid as the rocks it treads upon, it walks as fast as most horses trot, and it doesn't pull Cee's arms out of their sockets trying to charge up the trail behind a pack of strange horses in strange country. Not that she's found a mount with these collective attributes. That gives her an excuse to keep trading. It's an unspoken but well understood axiom at Willowcroft: if the equine turnover ever becomes static, so will Cee.

She's lost count of the trail rides she's entered since

her first in 1971. She's left her hoofprints in Wyoming, New Mexico and Nebraska as well as Colorado; she's ridden in snow and hail and in temperatures reaching 104 degrees. "I had so many clothes on I couldn't mount and had to be boosted up," she complained during one frigid ride. Another took place in a haven for rattlesnakes; they were even draped in the branches of the scrub oak. "Why am I doing this?" she questions periodically. Yet she has logged over 3500 miles on NATRC (National American Trail Riding Conference) rides, plus hundreds of miles spent conditioning, and has won countless cups, halters, buckets and ribbons, even a six pack of beer for being the oldest rider. "Which gripes the hell out of me," she grumbled. A silver cup for being the "most inspirational rider" was more to her liking.

In March of 1987 Cee was among 43 female athletes chosen as a Sportswoman of the Year by The Sportswomen of Colorado. At 79, she was easily the oldest as well as the smallest as she stood beside the 6'2" mistress of ceremonies, a basketball player, who presented her with a gold engraved medallion. But when the gathering of 600 rose to applaud her, Cee, in her red dress with the spotlight on her white hair, appeared as tall as her hostess. She accepted her award with poise and dignity although she had dreaded the event for weeks. High as she held her head that night, her feet, for once, were on the ground and not in a pair of stirrups.

Cee prefers competitive to endurance riding because, she claims, it's more of a challenge mentally and gives her more to work on during the year. An endurance ride is a straight-out race over 50 or 100 miles whereas a competitive ride is a timed event, covering 50 miles in two days. The horse is judged on condition, soundness, manners, and way of going. Horsemanship includes trail etiquette, presentation, equitation and stabling. The *rider's* soundness, conditioning and stabling are not considered.

"I'd never win as I couldn't push my horse that much. I've proved I can do 50 and I'll let it go at that," declared Cee after her first endurance ride in 1979 which she took at a fast trot. By 1984 she'd contradicted herself by putting seven more endurance rides under her saddle. Now, when she's weary with regulations imposed on competitive riding, she takes a break with endurance. "There's not so much to have to think about - you just go," she says.

Cee has learned the perils of the road, as well as the trail, since she took up her latest sport. Perched on the bench seat of her three quarter ton pickup, she drives with her chin in the air, straining to see over the top of the steering wheel. A camper on top provides her with the comforts of home, including a kitchen for TV dinners, and behind the truck, like an unwieldy barge, lurches the four-horse trailer. But the tires, eight in all, are a constant reminder to Cee that she was not born to be a trucker. There's hardly a trip without a flat tire or a mechanical failure of some sort. She's been left standing on the roadside with a flat tire, a dead engine, and burned out brakes. Her rig doesn't behave much better in camp, either. At night, with three or four horses tied to it, it shakes like a ship in heavy seas. When the horses are restless, Cee rolls out of her bunk several times a night in a futile effort to calm them.

One particularly sleepless night, she emerged at the crack of dawn to find her prize trail horse on its knees with three blankets over its head. On another ride, she pulled into camp late in a hard rain and parked in the first spot she found. In the middle of the night men with flashlights knocked on her camper and told her to clear out - there was a chance of floods. Cee refused; she was too tired to get dressed and go out again in the pouring rain. At 4:00 a.m. someone else knocked on the camper door and handed her the rope of her horse which had broken loose and was wandering around camp. In the morning Cee found that she was only twelve feet from the swollen creek; rivulets were running under her truck and some horses were up to their knees in water. Such nights are simply part of the game.

Often Cee and her friends start off the ride next day (30 miles the first, 20 miles the second day) with less than four hours uninterrupted sleep. The terrain is never easy; riders must climb and descend hills that would make a skier turn pale, clamber over downed timber, plow through rivers and slosh through bogs. There have been bad falls; Cee witnessed one where a horse slipped on a muddy slope and flipped end over end, nearly landing on its rider with each somersault. Sometimes they don't follow a trail at all but a series of ribbons, usually yellow, usually blending with the mountain flowers or yucca blossoms, and winding through forests and gullies that no clear-thinking horseman would consider traversing 100 years ago. Cee has been lost countless times. About every ten miles, horses are stopped for a vet check, and pulse and respiration are taken. If the animal is overtired or stressed, it is held back. Riders shift for themselves.

Cee has had her share of mishaps, a broken crupper, a saddle over the horse's head. She's been dumped in the middle of the river and ejected from a runaway in a field of thistles. And she's clung like a strange bird, poncho flapping, stirrups flopping, while her horse streaked across the prairie before slamming to a stop on the brink of a large ditch. All she lost that time was her boot in the bushes. One of the worst accidents happened in camp after a tough, twenty mile ride. Deciding to soak her mare's legs in a nearby stream, Cee jumped on bareback with only a rope and a halter for control. The mare took off bucking; the next thing Cee knew she was flat on her back in the camper where someone had carried her. A contingent of companions cancelled out of the ride to take Cee to the hospital. They pulled into Swedish at 3:30 a.m. with two rigs and four horses. Cee was sent home after the doctor decided she was reasonably sound, although her knee was the size of a cantaloupe.

"Boy oh boy am I sore today," she wrote. "Every time I move it's an effort. Charlie thinks Bruce is doing chores, Bruce thinks Charlie is, but I'm doing them as I must keep moving. I skipped lunch and marketing." She added, "I think it speaks pretty well for me not to break a bone - the doctor can scoff all he wants at my hormones, calcium and vitamin E pills. . . . Just don't let a doctor get his hands on you is my motto."

The people who make the trail riding circuit are, on the whole, there to enjoy the country as well as the competition. Cee has received a great deal of help and support from total strangers. A few, however, will go to extremes to win, though cash prizes are not given in competitive trail riding. Some have pushed their horses until the animals have gone lame or collapsed from exhaustion. Others have been caught shooting their horses with Butazolidan, a pain killer, and have left the ride rather than submit to blood tests.

Cee had a run-in of her own with "Fred," a rider with a reputation for spurring his horses up long hills until they broke down. As she passed through camp one evening, Cee saw Fred's horse tied to a trailer and Fred bent over its neck holding a flashlight. Cee stopped.

"What do you think he's doing?" asked Charlie Owen, who was with her.

"Be quiet. I wonder if he's giving it a shot."

"Did he?"

Cee waited a minute. "No," she said.

Shortly afterward the steward knocked on the door of her camper. He reported that several people had heard Cee say that Fred gave his horse a shot. "Pitcher ears in the dark," Cee snorted. Despite her denials, she was barred from riding the next day and so was Fred. He threatened to sue the management. Cee found herself face to face with Fred's irate wife who screamed that Cee had ruined her husband's career. When Cee confronted him to tell him the charges were unfounded, he threatened to sue her also. "I hope he does," was her response. "I've gathered enough evidence about how he treats his horses to hang him."

The upshot was a $250,000 suit for libel against Cynthia F. Wolf. Eighteen months later Cee, accompanied by Paul, had to appear for a deposition in downtown Denver, an area she hadn't seen in twenty years. She described it thus:

"I wore my grey suit and blouse and walked seven blocks from the United Bank building because your father got free parking. While we were sitting in the office where I was being briefed, the phone rang. When my lawyer got off he left the room for a moment, and when he came back he asked how was my pride?

"It seems the phone call was from Fred's lawyer who said Fred was willing to drop the suit if I would apologize. I said, 'Hell no, I have nothing to apologize for,' but I got such a dirty look from your father who of course was paying my lawyer fees, so I agreed I would. Mr. Johnson wrote a letter to the effect that I was sorry any embarrassment was caused by something I might have said that was misconstrued by some other party. It came to about three lines.

"I guess they either decided they didn't have a case or more likely Fred hadn't paid his lawyer, as the latter said if I didn't agree to that he'd drop the case, and Fred would have to get someone else. Maybe Fred thought he'd punished me enough to the tune of $1200 and getting down there at 9:00 a.m. in a dress. Why couldn't he have called the day before? Anyway, your father was much relieved as he painted dark pictures of me bankrupted and in jail. I'm afraid I didn't take it very seriously."

With Cee, things tend to travel in circles, much like a coyote. I remember riding as a child an old white mare called Hortense who every year, thanks to the matchmaking skills of my mother, produced a big mule foal. After a long hiatus, this curious hybrid has once again joined Cee's menagerie, in force. The mules at Willowcroft have even gone so far as to depose the horses, with the exception of Cee's ancient Arabian stallion Rouf, retired but not retiring.

I first got wind of Cee's latest enthusiasm when she announced in August of 1985 she had a "couple of neat riding mules." A few months later she wrote that her "Minnie," a 48 inch buckskin with striped legs and a lovely brown ribbon running from withers to tail, had

won for Cee a plaque, a two-pound belt buckle com-
memorating George Washington's Spanish jacks, and $40
at the National Western Stock Show. It was only a few
more months before the inevitable: Cee and Peggy
showed up at the first competitive ride of the season
mounted on mules.

Their appearance caused laughter and much skep-
ticism among the "horse people." The two little mules
didn't blink an eye but trudged 34 miles the first day.
Too tired to eat that night, they lay down as soon as they
were tied to the trailer which for once didn't rock. They
started fresh the next morning and earned 100 percent
each on soundness, manners and way of going. Cee won
second in horsemanship with a score of 98½, and Peggy's
mount won third, beating 15 Arabs in a ride fast enough
to eliminate 20 horses. One man was so intrigued with
Minnie he bought a picture of her. My mother's response
to victory was anything but humble.

"Dean Shrader told me I was a weirdo to get a mule
but retracted his words at the end of the ride and now
his wife wants one," she wrote. "I guess because there
were so many raised eyebrows I tried a little harder to
make the mules look good."

Her approach to muledom is, if anything, evan-
gelical. Currently she owns seven, four of which are
conditioned for competition, and she tries a little harder
with everyone, including her daughter, to present them
at their best. When I was at Willowcroft last, she handed
me Kate's rope with a mixture of enthusiasm and trepi-
dation. Kate is a brown mule with white socks and ears
that turn in at the tips when she shies. Kate at once
dragged me down the aisle of the barn. When I protested, Cee gave a little shrug and smiled.

"Oh, they all do that."

"Yes," Peggy chimed in. "When we first got them we were all flying after them like kites on a string."

If I fail to express my admiration for Kate - deep down I know she doesn't care a fig for me - I admit I rather like her. She is sure footed as a goat on the trail, no stumbling on a rock and skinning her nose. She walks, trots and canters like any horse, wades through streams, jumps logs, climbs mountains, leaps into the trailer and backs, at her own speed, out. I've viewed butterflies and even a golden eagle through her ears, those barometers of mule emotions, lopping loosely one moment, swinging forward to point out a deer or another suspicious object in the brush the next. When I get home, I don't have to curry Kate because she and her fellows always take a companionable and saluatory roll in the dust. Deep down, perhaps, I'm really a convert.

Or perhaps I like these small hoofed, dorsal striped animals because they've given my mother a different, if not new, lease on life. She's joined the Rocky Mountain Longears Conference and subscribes to *The Brayer*. She's made new friends and runs with a different crowd, the Wolf Pack, they call themselves. "Everybody wants to ride my mules," says Cee. Says Peggy, "Life at Willowcroft has gotten very active." I wonder when it wasn't but keep my mouth shut. I don't live here anymore, except, perhaps, in spirit. By taking on mules, Cee has also taken on a long tradition of ridicule and derision from those who view them as less than noble creatures. Cee will have to keep on trying a little harder. She doesn't mind. She'd be the first to say she can't turn down a challenge.

———————

I stand in Nana's doorway looking over the porch roof to the buildings and pasture beyond. I can make out Cee's small figure on a trajectory across the four acres. A cottonwood sapling has sprung up in the middle, and, as she passes it, I'm saddened because I know the tree will outlive my parents. I wish my daughter could know her grandmother in the same way I knew mine, that there were no spaces between generations. For a moment I wish I were my daughter's age, that the burdens and frustrations of growing older were magically erased, and like a film rewinding I could once again begin my childhood with all its small adventures and hazy expectations.

All night long the whistle of trains carrying coal from Wyoming to Texas has punctuated my sleep. The track runs through Littleton a mile away; the sound is from my girlhood, the high familiar hoot and rumble of passenger trains headed across the country. Last night I dreamt as I used to do when I was in college in Massachusetts, that I was riding a westbound train. In two weeks I'll return to the Adirondacks, but in my mind I will begin to move west again, back to Willowcroft, to a country I once knew. I have left the place of my birth and returned to it again and again, but time and distance have given me a gift; no longer do I see it as it is but as I want to see it. When Willowcroft is gone, I can still stand on the porch or at the door in Nana's room and look out through the cottonwoods, to the fields, to the mountains beyond. I will watch my mother cross the pasture. Of that, I'm glad. Like her, I tend to travel in circles.

"So what's next?" I ask after I've surveyed her crop of mules. Cee shrugs, her face crinkled, hair like a dandelion gone to seed. Her hazel eyes turn green as she laughs.

"I dunno. Zebras, maybe."

Alice Wolf Gilborn, a Colorado native, was born in Denver in 1936. She is a graduate of the Kent School, Wellesley College and the University of Delaware. Since 1972 she has lived in Blue Mountain Lake, New York, in the central Adirondacks, where she works as editor of publications for the Adirondack Museum and publishes a literary magazine, *Blueline*, dedicated to regional writing.